823.914 DOY

D1632750

BARTON PEVERIL COLLEGE LIBRARY
For renewals, please phone 023 80
This item must be returned on or before the last

1 3 FEB 2014
2 7 FEB 2014

Paddy
Clarke
Ha

Oxford
Literature
Companions

UNIVERSITY PRESS

Contents

BARTON PEVERIL
COLLEGE LIBRARY
EASTLEIGH SO50 5ZA

Introduction

What are Oxford Literature Companions?

Oxford Literature Companions is a series designed to provide you with comprehensive support for popular set texts. You can use the Companion alongside your novel, using relevant sections during your studies or using the book as a whole for revision.

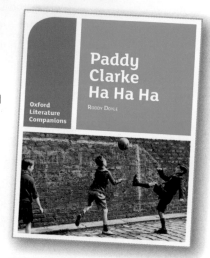

Each Companion includes detailed guidance and practical activities on:

- **Plot and Structure**
- **Context**
- **Characters**
- **Language**
- **Themes**
- **Skills and Practice**

How does this book help with exam preparation?

As well as providing guidance on key areas of the novel, throughout this book you will also find 'UpGrade' features. These are tips to help with your exam preparation and performance.

In addition, in the extensive **Skills and Practice** chapter, the **Exam skills** section provides detailed guidance on areas such as how to prepare for the exam, understanding the question, planning your response and hints for what to do (or not do) in the exam.

In the **Skills and Practice** chapter there is also a bank of **Sample questions** and **Sample answers**. The **Sample answers** are marked and include annotations and a summative comment.

How does this book help with terminology?

Throughout the book, key terms are **highlighted** in the text and explained on the same page. There is also a detailed **Glossary** at the end of the book that explains, in the context of the novel, all the relevant literary terms highlighted in this book.

Which edition of the novel has this book used?

Where there are page references in this book, they refer to the Vintage Books edition of *Paddy Clarke Ha Ha Ha* (ISBN 978-0-749-39735-7).

How does this book work?

Each book in the Oxford Literature Companions series follows the same approach and includes the following features:

- **Key quotations** from the novel
- **Key terms** explained on the page and linked to a complete glossary at the end of the book
- **Activity boxes** to help improve your understanding of the novel
- **UpGrade** tips to help prepare you for your exam

To help illustrate the features in this book, here are two annotated pages taken from this Oxford Literature Companion:

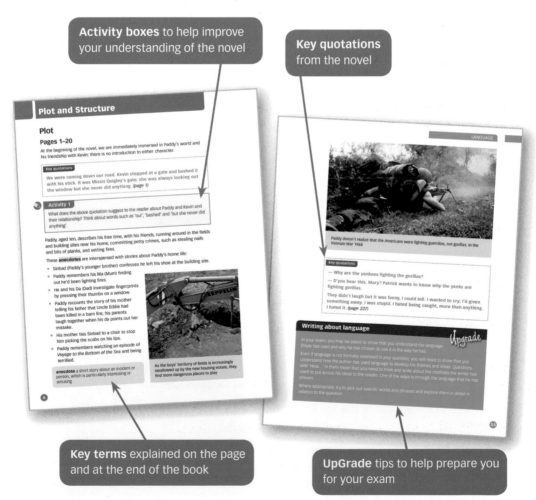

Activity boxes to help improve your understanding of the novel

Key quotations from the novel

Plot and Structure

Plot

Pages 1–20

At the beginning of the novel, we are immediately immersed in Paddy's world and his friendship with Kevin; there is no introduction to either character.

Key quotations

We were coming down our road. Kevin stopped at a gate and bashed it with his stick. It was Missis Quigley's gate; she was always looking out the window but she never did anything. *(page 1)*

Activity 1

What does the above quotation suggest to the reader about Paddy and Kevin and their relationship? Think about words such as 'our', 'bashed' and 'but she never did anything'.

Paddy, aged ten, describes his free time, with his friends, running around in the fields and building sites near his home, committing petty crimes, such as stealing nails and bits of planks, and setting fires.

These **anecdotes** are interspersed with stories about Paddy's home life:

- Sinbad (Paddy's younger brother) confesses he left his shoe at the building site.
- Paddy remembers his Ma (Mum) finding out he'd been lighting fires.
- He and his Da (Dad) investigate fingerprints by pressing their thumbs on a window.
- Paddy recounts the story of his mother telling his father that Uncle Eddie had been killed in a barn fire; his parents laugh together when his da points out her mistake.
- His mother ties Sinbad to a chair to stop him picking the scabs on his lips.
- Paddy remembers watching an episode of *Voyage to the Bottom of the Sea* and being terrified.

anecdote a short story about an incident or person, which is particularly interesting or amusing

As the boys' territory of fields is increasingly swallowed up by the new housing estate, they find more dangerous places to play

LANGUAGE

Paddy doesn't realize that the Americans were fighting guerrillas, not gorillas, in the Vietnam War 1968

Key quotations

— Why are the yankees fighting the gorillas?

— D'you hear this, Mary? Patrick wants to know why the yanks are fighting gorillas.

They didn't laugh but it was funny, I could tell. I wanted to cry; I'd given something away. I was stupid. I hated being caught, more than anything. I hated it. *(page 227)*

Writing about language

Upgrade

In your exam, you may be asked to show that you understand the language Doyle has used and why he has chosen to use it in the way he has.

Even if language is not formally assessed in your question, you will need to show that you understand how the author has used language to develop his themes and ideas. Questions with 'How...' in them mean that you need to think and write about the methods the writer has used to put across his ideas to the reader. One of the ways is through the language that he has chosen.

Where appropriate, try to pick out specific words and phrases and explore them in detail in relation to the question.

Key terms explained on the page and at the end of the book

UpGrade tips to help prepare you for your exam

Plot

Pages 1–20

At the beginning of the novel, we are immediately immersed in Paddy's world and his friendship with Kevin; there is no introduction to either character.

> **Key quotations**
>
> **We were coming down our road. Kevin stopped at a gate and bashed it with his stick. It was Missis Quigley's gate; she was always looking out the window but she never did anything.** *(page 1)*

Activity 1

What does the above quotation suggest to the reader about Paddy and Kevin, and their relationship? Think about words such as 'our', 'bashed' and 'but she never did anything'.

Paddy, aged ten, describes his free time with his friends, running around in the fields and building sites near his home, committing petty crimes, such as stealing nails and bits of planks, and setting fires.

These **anecdotes** are interspersed with stories about Paddy's home life:

- Sinbad (Paddy's younger brother) confesses he left his shoe at the building site.
- Paddy remembers his Ma (Mum) finding out he'd been lighting fires.
- He and his Da (Dad) investigate fingerprints by pressing their thumbs on a window.
- Paddy recounts the story of his mother telling his father that Uncle Eddie had been killed in a barn fire; his parents laugh together when his Da points out her mistake.
- His mother ties Sinbad to a chair to stop him picking the scabs on his lips.
- Paddy remembers watching an episode of *Voyage to the Bottom of the Sea* and being terrified.

anecdote a short story about an incident or person, which is particularly interesting or amusing

As the boys' territory of fields is increasingly swallowed up by the new housing estate, they find more dangerous places to play

Activity 2

Paddy's parents' marriage is one of the important narrative threads through the novel. Keep track of key moments that show how their relationship changes by completing the PEE (Point, Evidence, Explanation) table below.

Point	Evidence	Explanation
Paddy tells his mother what Kevin said about Mister O'Connell.	'My ma said that he did it [cried] because he missed his wife. [...] My da agreed with her.' (page 3)	Paddy's parents seem to make a good team, as his father simply supports his wife's sympathetic explanation of Mister O'Connell's sadness.
Paddy's ma tells his da that Uncle Eddie has been killed in the barn fire but his father replies that Uncle Eddie did not mention that he was dead when they walked up the road together.	'There was a gap and then they burst out laughing, the two of them.' (page 14)	The good humour and closeness of Paddy's parents, shown through 'the two of them', highlights their happiness.

Pages 20–33

There is a description of Miss Watkins, the teacher before Mister Hennessey. Paddy describes the day that she read out the Proclamation of Independence on the 50 year anniversary of the Easter Rising. She hits Paddy three times on each hand for lying that the Thomas Clarke in the picture is his grandfather. This is the first explicit reference to corporal punishment in the novel.

Paddy and his father discuss the book his father is reading, *The Naked and the Dead*.

After going to buy his father's newspaper, Paddy becomes concerned about the front-page article, which has the headline, 'World War Three Looms Near'. There ensues a long conversation with his father about the military tensions between Israel and its immediate neighbours.

Activity 3

1. Why do you think Doyle includes the conversation about World War Three between Paddy and his father? What purpose does it serve? What do we learn from it?

2. Why do you think this scene concludes with the lines: 'We had our dinner. It was lovely. The mince wasn't too runny. I sat in the chair beside Da, Sinbad's chair. Sinbad said nothing' (page 30)?

Paddy and Sinbad write letters to Santa and even though Paddy no longer believes in him he keeps quiet and does not reveal the truth to Sinbad. These closing lines to this section of the novel seem to hint that Paddy's life is changing: he is growing up and there seems to be unrest in his family and the wider world.

> **Key quotations**
>
> I jumped on Sinbad's [hot water] bottle. Nothing happened. I didn't do it again. Sometimes when nothing happened it was really getting ready to happen. *(page 33)*

Pages 34–41

These pages of the novel are mostly concerned with Liam and Aidan's life. Paddy describes Liam and Aidan's house and explains why he prefers it to his own.

A few pages on, Paddy describes Liam and Aidan's auntie and then a woman called Margaret who is not a relation, but is also referred to as an auntie. We find out that she is Mister O'Connell's girlfriend and all the boys are quite intrigued by her.

Other anecdotes that Paddy tells the reader include:

* Paddy tells Ian McEvoy a comment his mother made about Ian's mother and confesses to us that he does not really understand what he is saying.
* He describes how he pushes his sandwiches under his desk at school and then recalls a mealtime at home one day when Sinbad wouldn't eat his dinner: 'He [Sinbad and Paddy's Da] made Sinbad sit there for an hour until he was ready to inspect the plate. It was empty; in me and in the bin' *(page 37)*.

Don't just retell the story of the novel in your exam. Instead, select information relevant to the particular question being asked.

Upgrade

Pages 41–61

Paddy's parents' rows and tense silences are explicitly mentioned for the first time when Paddy hears them arguing but thinks it is burglars. Although it is the first direct reference to their arguments, Paddy states, 'They were having another of their fights' *(page 42)*, which gives us the impression that this has become a regular event. Throughout these 20 pages, the reader's attention is drawn to the increasingly frequent moments of awkwardness within the family home, although Paddy does not understand what is happening and thinks it is his fault.

> **Key quotations**
>
> I didn't know what had happened. I didn't know what I'd done. *(page 53)*

As his home life becomes increasingly difficult, so Paddy's tendency to regurgitate facts from the world around him increases. He retells the story of Father Damien and the lepers. He lists facts, such as, **'Snails and slugs were gastropods [...] Association football was played with a round ball on a rectangular pitch by two sides of eleven people. [...] Geronimo was the last of the renegade Apaches'** *(page 53).* Paddy appears to retreat into a world of facts when he finds the emotional aspect of his life difficult to bear.

Paddy and his friends continue to torment one another and their neighbours, and he gives a long description of a couple called Mister and Missis Kiernan who sound young and ambitious: **'They weren't old. They both went to work, in his car. She drove it as well'** *(pages 58–59).* Paddy cannot understand why they do not have children and so dismisses the answer to the query with **'That's stupid'** *(page 58).* Paddy and his friends get into the Kiernans' garden and take it in turns to headbutt Missis Kiernan's knickers hanging on the washing line. When he then sees Missis Kiernan in the local shop he is convinced she knows what they all did and even when back home he worries that she is about to ring the doorbell and expose his crime to his parents.

Activity 4

1. Using the text as your guide, describe Mister and Missis Kiernan in detail.

2. With a partner, discuss why Doyle (the author) has chosen to **juxtapose** the anecdote about the Kiernans with the increasing discomfort and tension of Paddy's home life.

Other information from this section of the novel includes:

- Paddy's father flushes a mouse down the toilet while the family look on with a mixture of interest and horror.

- Paddy makes his own hosts (Communion wafers) from Vienna roll and Batch bread. He tells his parents he has a vocation.

- Paddy, Sinbad and their gang of friends draw big Vs on their chests and call themselves the Vigour tribe.

- Paddy describes his visits to the Baldoyle library with his father.

juxtaposition various things or ideas placed side by side to highlight the differences between them

Pages 61–83

In these pages Paddy makes a number of references to violence of various sorts:

- Ian McEvoy goes to sleep in class and Mister Hennessey hits him.
- Kevin once poked Paddy in the eye in the style of *The Three Stooges*.
- Luke Cassidy once had an epileptic fit during the Friday school 'cinema'.
- Liam breaks his teeth playing Grand National, in which the boys run through various neighbours' gardens.
- Kevin breaks Missis Quigley's toilet window and Paddy is banished to his bedroom after she complains to his parents, although his father does not punish him further: **'Things were going well. He wasn't in the right mood, when he wanted to hit me. He was being fair'** *(page 79)*.

Activity 5

As you read the novel, make a note of all the types of violence Paddy describes in the three environments of home, school and friends. Think carefully about whether one form of violence increases as another decreases and what Doyle's purpose is in depicting Paddy's experiences in this way.

Pages 83–103

The tension created by Paddy's father is further explored in this section of the novel after he hits Paddy for failing to sing a song correctly. Afterwards Paddy says, **'He put his hand on my shoulder, the other one. I wanted to squirm it away but after a while I didn't mind'** *(page 89)*.

Later, he describes his father accusing first Sinbad and then him of scratching one of his records and his mother defends them both. Paddy explains, **'My face burned when I was waiting for something else to happen, for him to say something back to her'** *(page 90)*.

Paddy's feelings towards his father are quite ambivalent (mixed) at this point. When he buys a car and lets Paddy and his friends sit in the back of it while he reverses up the road, Paddy exclaims, **'Da sang the Batman music, he was mad sometimes, brilliant mad'** *(page 90)*.

However, tensions rise again when the family go on a picnic in the new car; his parents have a row and his mother gets out of the car into pouring rain.

Activity 6

Why might the failed picnic be seen as a key point in the novel?

Other events in this section of the novel include:

- At school, the class have to line up for a medical examination. When Paddy goes in for the examination with Kevin, he sees that Kevin has a dirty mark in his pants but he decides not to tell him.

- Paddy and his family visit his aunts and uncles after Sinbad's Holy Communion.

- Paddy also tells us about Father Moloney, who visits his class every month for religious discussions. He recalls one in which they discussed death, heaven, Limbo and Purgatory. In his recollections, Doyle shows us Paddy's childish understanding of sin and punishment when he says, **'It was about a million years for every venial sin, depending on the sin and if you'd done it before and promised that you wouldn't do it again'** *(page 84)*.

Pages 103–125

In this section, Paddy describes the changing landscape around his house; the uncertainties of the present are a stark contrast to Paddy's memory of a time when he was small enough to sit under the dining-room table, before Cathy and Deirdre were born and when Sinbad could only crawl.

In this ever-decreasing territory, Paddy's adventures with his friends seem to get wilder and sometimes even more dangerous:

- Paddy and his friends climb into a new water pipe that is being laid for the new houses and factories that are being built. Kevin waits in it rather than running through and Paddy's pleased that he finds him: **'This was me and Kevin together. The two of us went deeper into the pipe so the others wouldn't see us'** *(page 107)*. Paddy enjoys being Kevin's friend but, at the end of this scene, he reveals: **'he pruned me'** *(page 108)*.

- The boys push Aidan down a manhole and throw mud at him.

- They look for ice-pop sticks in the road so they can dig at the new tar.

- Ian McEvoy is badly injured by a wire booby trap that was not set by the boys. They decide it was set by someone from one of the new Corporation houses. When Paddy refers to them as **'Slum scum'** his mother hits him: **'She never hit me usually but she did then. She smacked behind my head'** *(page 118)*.

- Paddy and his friends play football but he argues with Ian McEvoy about being in goal. However, when one of the children from the Corporation houses offers to go in goal he responds with: **'This is our field, I said again. I kicked him'** *(page 121)*.

- The boys build huts out of sods of earth and lay booby traps to defend them.

We also gain a glimpse into the lives of older boys in Barrytown, with the description of Kevin's older brother and friends.

- Through the window of Kevin's house they watched Kevin's brother and friends playing Scalextric.

- Paddy describes Kevin's brother, Martin, and recalls that he **'got into big trouble once'** *(page 114)*.

- Martin also attacked Sinbad once: painting the other lens of his glasses black and making him walk home with a white stick.

At the end of this section of the novel, the sudden violence from Paddy's mother is shocking and unexpected: when Paddy returns from digging at the road he has tar on his trousers so his mother makes him take them off. While his trousers are down, **'She slapped the side of my leg'** *(page 125).*

Pages 125–145

Paddy's father is becoming increasingly aggressive to his mother: **'He made his hand open and close like a beak, the fingers stiff, right into her face. — Nag nag nag'** *(pages 125–126).* The children walk in during the argument.

Paddy sees this aggression and senses the increasing tension in the house. His father's behaviour leads Paddy to be more protective of his brother, even lying about a boy being sick to divert attention away from Sinbad when his father is about to punish him.

Activity 7

What do you think Paddy means when he says about his lie: 'I'd won. I'd saved Sinbad'? *(page 126)*

Paddy increasingly comments on the tensions in the family home although his understanding of it comes later. He describes receiving a football book for his birthday with George Best's autograph in it. He does not realize that the autograph is a print and thanks his father, who remains quiet about the truth.

Key quotations

A year after that I knew that it wasn't George Best's real autograph at all; it was only printing and my da was a liar. *(page 137)*

The violence of the games Paddy plays with his friends also seems to increase. He describes a ritualistic ceremony around a fire in which they chant 'bad' words and Kevin, acting as high priest, hits them with a poker. Liam deserts the game after Kevin hits him twice and Paddy reports that Smiffy O'Rourke left the week before after having been hit on the back five times.

In contrast to these violent and tense situations, Paddy comments on a number of events that obviously bring him happiness and comfort:

- He celebrates George Best's goal in the European Cup Final by running around the garden.
- He recounts a conversation with his mother about the meaning of 'drawing room', about his name and about wanting to go to Africa to see the animals when he's older.

Pages 145–165

This section begins with three short anecdotes:

- the description of the marrowfat peas
- Da's joke, which Paddy does not understand
- Sinbad and Paddy knocking on their parents' bedroom door too early to get up.

Activity 8

Why does Doyle write about seemingly insignificant events like these?

The landscape is becoming increasingly built up and Paddy and his friends are playing on smaller and smaller patches of land, as well as building sites that used to be fields.

- Paddy loses his big toenail on a piece of scaffolding left on a building site.
- Paddy and his friends build a wigwam on their territory and Mister O'Connell mistakenly calls it an igloo.
- The boys cycle around another new, unfinished, housing estate and climb on the roofs of blocks of garages.
- In a bid to retain control of the territory, the boys try to rule the new estate. They make a young boy climb on to a garage roof and then hold him over the side and kick him. The boys also go 'knick-knacking' (knocking on doors and running away).
- Paddy and his friends shoplift from **'about six shops between Raheny and Baldoyle'** *(page 156)*.

> **Key quotations**
>
> … **the people in the shops were friends with our parents. They'd all got married and moved to Barrytown at the same time.** *(page 157)*

Other events in this section include:

- Paddy and Kevin count all the Venetian blinds in Barrytown. Paddy watches his mother washing the ones in their house: **'She only ever did it once'** *(page 164)*.
- Paddy remembers when his Uncle Raymond brought over a bed for Sinbad.
- His parents' arguments become more frequent and open, although Paddy thinks Sinbad is unaware of them.
- At the end of this part of the novel, Paddy describes his mother listening to the radio. He sits with her, but he watches her rather than listening.

Activity 9

Bayside is a more modern housing estate with a different, and new, layout. Describe the estate and consider why Doyle includes details about it. What does it show us about Paddy's environment?

Pages 165–180

The boys play football across the road because **'Our pitch was gone'** *(page 165)*. Paddy explains the hierarchy of the friendship group through the way they choose names for themselves. Aidan commentates as they play. The game has few rules and throughout the boys argue and hurl abuse at one another: **'This always happened as well'** *(page 169)*.

Paddy and his friends play football in the street after their pitch has gone

Paddy spins round and round and describes the sensation of dizziness. This leads him on to thinking about being sick if you'd just eaten your dinner, about the fact that swimming is dangerous immediately after eating and that someone might give you the kiss of life. He thinks kissing is stupid and then recalls the one time he was sick after spinning. When Paddy gets up in the morning he sees that the table has not been cleared from the night before. He comments: **'It was stupid, not doing the dishes in the night [...] Now, though, she was going to have rub real hard. Loads of elbow grease. Blood, sweat and tears. She'd have her work cut out for her. It served her right'** *(page 176).*

Activity 10

When Paddy sees the dishes, he says 'It was stupid' and 'It served her right'. Although it's Paddy narrating the story, where do you think he has got this attitude from? Why might he express these views?

> **Key quotations**
>
> **Something happened when I was asking it; it was in my voice, a difference between the beginning and the end. The reason – it fell into me. The reason she hadn't done the dishes. I'd been in a lift once – twice – up, then down. This was like going down. I nearly didn't finish: I knew the answer. It unwrapped while I was talking. The reason.** *(page 178)*

Activity 11

Why does Doyle write about Paddy spinning around until he's dizzy, followed by more examples of his parents fighting?

Pages 180–196

This section of the novel shows how confused Paddy feels about his own friendships and loyalties. He explains how much he hated it when he was put beside David Geraghty one week, but then he realized how much fun David was and enjoyed himself: **'I sometimes hoped that I'd be put beside David Geraghty again but I was always glad when I wasn't'** *(page 183)*.

Two of the boys from the Corporation houses, Charles Leavy and Seán Whelan, join Paddy's class. Paddy feels animosity towards them and is delighted when Seán is put beside Liam as **'It was great. Liam was finished now'** *(page 181)*.

Paddy is hit by Mister Hennessey when he watches Seán Whelan rather than concentrating on the lesson. Paddy determines to get his revenge on Seán, who he blames, and says, **'He'd be easy to get. He wouldn't hit back. I'd get him. He wasn't rough looking'** *(page 183)*. However, Paddy is surprised when the fight happens because Kevin pushes him into Seán beyond the confines of the school gate and Charles Leavy steps in and kicks Paddy: **'No one jumped in. No one said anything'** *(page 186)*.

The boys run away when a workman intervenes, but Paddy recognizes that there has been a shift in his friendship group.

> **Key quotations**
>
> **No one had jumped in for me when Charles Leavy had been going to kill me; it took me a while to get used to that, to make it make sense. To make it alright. The quiet, the waiting. All of them looking. Kevin standing beside Seán Whelan. Looking.** *(pages 186–187)*

Paddy's fight with Charles Leavy has a profound effect on him

We see Paddy's relationship with Sinbad changing as his parents' marriage falters:

- Paddy locks Sinbad in a suitcase but then becomes frightened and calls his father to rescue his brother.
- He decides to start using Sinbad's real name – Francis.
- Sinbad does not want the night light on any more and Paddy is unable to say that he wants it on: **'He turned off the light and I was trapped in the full dark'** *(page 189).*
- Paddy finds his father about to hit Sinbad for putting sugar in a neighbour's petrol tank but he changes his mind when Sinbad cries and Paddy sings to deflect attention.

Paddy's father's violence towards his mother grows and Paddy hears him hit her, although he cannot make sense of it. He starts guarding his mother: he stays awake at night and pretends he has a lot of homework so that he can remain near his parents in the evenings. Paddy does not understand what is happening: **'I loved him'** *(page 191).*

Key quotations

He'd hit her. Across the face; smack. I tried to imagine it. It didn't make sense. I'd heard it; he'd hit her. She'd come out of the kitchen, straight up to their bedroom.

Across the face. *(page 190)*

> ### Activity 12
>
> What do you notice about the sentence structure that Doyle uses when Paddy describes hearing his father hit his mother?

Other events in this section of the novel include:

- Paddy moves to the front desk at school.
- Aidan gets stuck in a trench and the boys wonder if you can drown in mud. Liam fetches his father and a ladder and Aidan is saved.
- A boy called Keith Simpson drowns in a pond in a field where the building work has not started. His death affects the whole town. Paddy comments, **'Da hugged Ma when he came home'** *(page 195)*.
- Everyone goes to the funeral and the children have the rest of the day off school.
- Paddy lies and tells his friends that Keith Simpson was his cousin.

Pages 196–225

Paddy and his friends discuss 'hari-kiri', a form of Japanese ritual suicide. Paddy contemplates different methods of suicide.

The boys try to steal sawdust for Ian McEvoy's guinea pig, but they are caught. When the guinea pig dies of cold, the boys, believing it's Mrs McEvoy's fault, get a doll and stick pins in it to take their revenge. They push the dead guinea pig through Missis Kilmartin's letterbox.

Paddy is now quite preoccupied with the relationship between his father and mother. He comments, **'She listened to him much more than he listened to her'** *(page 202)*.

He begins to consider his father's behaviour in much more depth. Initially he explains, **'Fathers were like that, all the fathers I knew'** *(page 203)* but then afterwards, **'Sometimes he was just being mean'** *(page 203)*. When Paddy wins a medal for running, he tries to show his father but is initially met with, **'Get out; not now'** (page 204). Although his father calls him back and takes an interest, Paddy **'wished he'd done it the first time. It wasn't fair the way he made you nearly cry before he changed and did what you wanted him to'** *(page 205)*. Paddy recognizes that his father is sometimes mindlessly cruel.

Paddy considers the main terms that parents use to punish their children: **'I'll crucify you. [...] I'll leather you. I'll skin you alive. I'll break every bone in your body. I'll tear you limb from limb. I'll maim you. [...] I'll swing for you'** *(page 206)*.

Activity 13

Look at Paddy's description of his parents reading, from 'Da's face was different when he was reading the paper' to 'I hated him for doing it' *(page 208).*

Immediately after this section, what does Paddy describe newspapers as? Why?

Paddy's mother and father have a tense conversation, which Paddy repeats to the reader. He tries to intervene by asking if he can watch television and manages to make his parents laugh before he is sent to bed. The conversation is a series of short questions and answers, which reflect how difficult the atmosphere is, but at the end of it Paddy is pleased with his achievement: **'I wanted to go while it was nice. I'd made it like that'** *(page 211).*

Sinbad is humiliated in front of Paddy's class by Mister Hennessey, who tells Paddy to take Sinbad's work home to show his mother. Afterwards Paddy reassures Sinbad that he won't tell her what happened.

Paddy's parents' arguments and fights intensify. One morning Paddy's mother does not get up and, although his father tells him she's sick, Paddy senses that something more has happened when his father deters him from going in to see her: **'He didn't want me to. There was something'** *(page 215).*

In the evening, Paddy delays going home and dawdles with Liam and Aidan. When he does get in his mother is up but still in her dressing gown. The next morning she still does not get dressed and, although Paddy wants to believe it's because she had not got dressed 'yet' and is better, he writes, **'She looked straighter. She moved quicker'** *(page 219)* suggesting that something more sinister had happened to her.

> **Key quotations**
>
> **They were fighting all the time now. They said nothing but it was a fight. The way he folded his paper and snapped it, he was saying something. The way she got up when one of the girls was crying upstairs, sighed and stooped, wanting him to see that she was tired. It was happening.** *(pages 221–222)*
>
> **But she wasn't cuddling us; she was hanging on to us.** *(page 222)*

Paddy tries to talk to Sinbad about their parents' fights when the boys are in bed and their parents are still downstairs, but Sinbad insists that their parents are talking rather than arguing. In the morning Paddy tries to help Sinbad, but his brother is too cautious that it is a trick and will not accept Paddy's help. This in turn irritates Paddy although he insists: **'I didn't hit him'** *(page 225).*

Paddy describes the latest craze at school: either saying you 'kneed' someone, meaning to have given them a dead leg, or asking if you are 'boring' them, and then digging your finger in their ribs. He is surprised that Charles Leavy does not do it to anybody.

Activity 14

Paddy writes, 'You wanted to show off in front of Charles Leavy. You wanted to say bad words. You wanted him to look at you the proper way' *(page 225)*.

Why does Doyle show Paddy becoming increasingly impressed by Charles Leavy and his behaviour as his parents' marriage falls apart?

Pages 226–244

Paddy sits with his parents while they watch the news. There is an air of tension all the time in the house, although he reports, **'They said nothing for long bits but that wasn't bad; they were watching television or reading, or my ma was doing a hard bit of knitting. It didn't make me nervous; their faces were okay'** *(page 226)*. Paddy reports their arguments in terms of not having them and of not talking. There is no longer any real happiness or quiet contentment.

Paddy describes the news he sees on television but misunderstands and thinks the Americans are fighting gorillas rather than guerrillas. He is ashamed when his father teases him without laughing.

Paddy asks Kevin if his parents argue but then regrets having the conversation with him rather than having it with Liam as Kevin asks too many questions. Paddy ends up making up a story about an aunt and uncle fighting.

Mister Hennessey accuses Paddy of being allowed to stay up late and watch television and threatens to telephone his mother. Paddy confides in us that he has been making himself stay awake all night after hearing his father laugh when his mother screamed **'in a way that meant nothing funny'** *(page 233)*.

Later, Paddy falls asleep in class and wakes up to find himself in the headmaster's office. When Paddy returns to class, Mister Hennessey is kind to everyone for the rest of the day. His questioning of Paddy after school reveals that he has more insight into the situation than Paddy is aware of.

All Paddy's friends want to be near him and help him, but inwardly Paddy identifies much more with Charles Leavy: **'Charles Leavy didn't care. He was the only one that knew what had happened'** *(page 238)*.

Paddy feels isolated from his friends and feels the need to protect his family.

Paddy's parents fill the silences in their relationship by watching television

Key quotations

They were all there, and I didn't like them much. I was alone. [...] I realised something funny; I wanted to be with Sinbad. *(page 239)*

Paddy tries to show his love for Sinbad by giving him his biscuit, but Sinbad is so used to being tricked that he refuses it and Paddy tries to force it in his mouth. Paddy explains to us that he wants Sinbad **'to know; he had to get ready like me. I wanted to be able to stand beside him'** *(page 242)*.

Paddy's father comes home drunk one evening. Paddy recognizes a change in him but still cannot comprehend it.

Key quotations

I couldn't prove it. I sometimes didn't believe it; I'd really think that there was nothing wrong – the way they were chatting and drinking their tea, the way we all looked at the television – but I'd swing back again before happiness could trap me. She was lovely. He was nice. *(page 244)*

Paddy recognizes that his father is probably having an affair even though: **'There was no proof'** *(page 245)*.

Activity 15

Read the passage on page 245 from 'Mister O'Driscoll...' to ' ... I was going to be ready.'

What do you think Paddy meant by 'I was going to be ready'?

Pages 245–265

Paddy and Kevin play football with Charles Leavy and Seán Whelan, and Paddy watches their friendship carefully: **'They were laughing, pushing each other, trying to trip each other up. The next time Kevin got the ball I pretended I was trying to trip him, and he kicked me'** *(page 247)*.

Activity 16

Describe Charles Leavy's house (as mentioned on page 249) and why Paddy says, 'I wanted to go in there and be liked' *(page 249)*.

Paddy smokes with Charles Leavy and is rude about Kevin to him.

> **Key quotations**
>
> I felt good. I'd started. I looked across at Kevin. I didn't miss him. I was afraid though. I'd no one now. The way I'd wanted it. *(page 253)*

Paddy listens all the time now to his parents' arguments, shouting and tears. He claims he is preparing himself for either his mother or father leaving. He considers his parents' fights but accepts that he does not understand why they do not get on. A lot of Paddy's comments are filled with fear and tension – desperation to maintain the fragile peace of an evening: **'I didn't want to disturb him. [...] I hoped it was a brilliant book. [...] I listened on the landing. [...] I listened'** *(page 259)*. He prepares to run away from home.

Paddy's relationship with Sinbad has changed dramatically.

> **Key quotations**
>
> He'd found out; he'd found out. I'd wanted him to talk because I was scared. Pretending to be protecting him, I'd wanted him close to me, to share, to listen together; to stop it or run away. He knew: I was frightened and lonely, more than he was. *(page 260)*

Paddy tries to speak to his brother about their parents on the way to school, but Sinbad refuses to talk to him.

He compares his mother to all the others he knows and decides she is the best.

Paddy compares Mister Hennessey and Miss Watkins' teaching methods; he concludes that neither is enjoyable. Paddy comments, **'We laughed. We had to'** *(page 265)*.

Pages 265–282

Paddy wakes in the morning to discover that his father has not been home all night, although his mother pretends he has already left for work.

Paddy follows Charles Leavy out of school during break time. He tries to talk to Charles about running away and then imagines what it would be like. He is desperate to find a way to bring his parents back together. Back at school, Paddy and Kevin kick and hit each other while lining up at the end of break.

> **Key quotations**
>
> I didn't care. He hadn't hurt me bad. Anyway, I could get him back. He wasn't my friend any more. He was a sap, a spoofer and a liar. He hadn't a clue. *(page 271)*

Activity 17

Paddy and Kevin have a fight in the schoolyard. Why do you think Doyle describes it in such detail?

Paddy is 'boycotted' by all his friends; only David Geraghty speaks to him. Then one break, David thumps him on the back with one of his crutches and, through tears, says, **'Kevin said to give you that'** *(page 280)*.

Paddy's father leaves after Paddy sees him hit his mother.

> **Key quotations**
>
> — **Paddy Clarke** –
>
> **Paddy Clarke** –
>
> **Has no da.**
>
> **Ha ha ha!** *(page 281)*

Paddy's father comes to visit on Christmas Eve. His father shakes his hand and asks him how he is. Paddy replies formally and politely, with the final lines of the novel: ' — **Very well, thank you'** *(page 282)*.

Activity 18

Why do you think Doyle gave his novel the title *Paddy Clarke Ha Ha Ha* when we only find out its true meaning on the penultimate (second last) page of the story?

Structure

Paddy Clarke Ha Ha Ha is a **retrospective narrative** told in the **first person**: Paddy, a child of ten, is the **narrator**.

The narrative structure of the novel is unusual. It does not follow the conventional structure of a story (introduction, complication, climax, resolution). Instead, it is a series of interwoven anecdotes or **vignettes**. Unlike most novels, it is not broken down into chapters or other parts and much of Paddy's narrative jumps about, both between the past and the present and between one anecdote and another, much as a person's thoughts do.

However, even though the narrative does not follow a **linear** pattern, underlying all the interwoven stories are two strong narrative threads – the story of Paddy and his friends and the story of Paddy's parents' marriage – both of which are told **chronologically**. It is also possible for us to gain a sense of the passing of time as we see how Barrytown gradually changes.

The narrative structure may be confusing to begin with, but remember that Doyle uses it deliberately in order to achieve a particular effect: it makes the novel seem more like a series of memories.

chronological/linear narrative the presentation of events in a story in the order in which they actually occurred

first-person narrative a story told from the narrator's point of view, using the pronoun 'I' or 'me'

narrator the person who tells a story (Paddy is the narrator in *Paddy Clarke Ha Ha Ha*)

retrospective narrative a narrative relating events that happened in the narrator's past

vignette a short, descriptive sketch that creates an impression of a character, setting or concept

Writing about plot and structure

Upgrade

You will need to know your way confidently around the plot of the novel. This means that you need to be able to trace a theme or character right the way through the novel, rather than just writing about one specific part. However, always ensure you are answering the exam question and not just retelling the story in your answer!

As well as the events of the novel, you need to be able to write about the structure to get good marks. This means that you will need to show that you understand that Doyle chose to use specific techniques to develop his novel. This might include writing about:

- his choice of narrator
- his decision to use a child's voice
- his decision not to structure the novel using chapters or other dividers
- the effect he achieves by writing in a series of anecdotes.

Context

The context of a novel relates to the time in which it was written or the time in which it is set. For example, if you study Charles Dickens's *Oliver Twist*, published in serial format from 1837, you might consider the relevance of the introduction of the Poor Law in England in 1834 on Dickens's opinions and writing.

Paddy Clarke Ha Ha Ha was first published in 1993 but is set in the late 1960s. It is useful, therefore, to think about why that period of time might be of interest to Roddy Doyle and how he evokes (creates in our minds) the setting for his readers.

Biography of Roddy Doyle

- Doyle was born in Dublin, Ireland in 1958.
- He grew up in Kilbarrack, a suburb north of Dublin.
- After graduating from university, Doyle became a teacher in a school north of Dublin.
- He currently lives in Dublin with his wife and children.
- Doyle is the author of nine novels, a collection of stories and a memoir of his parents.
- He has also written five books for children.
- He has written for the stage, including co-writing an adaptation of his novel *The Woman Who Walked into Doors*.
- He wrote the screenplays for a number of his stories including *The Snapper* and *The Van*.
- He co-wrote the screenplay for his most successful screen adaptation, *The Commitments*.
- *Paddy Clarke Ha Ha Ha* won the Booker Prize in 1993.

Roddy Doyle (1958–) has written several novels based in fictional Barrytown, including *Paddy Clarke Ha Ha Ha* and *The Commitments*, which was made into a film

Mention the writer's background only in relation to how it may have affected what he shows in the novel.

Historical and cultural context of the novel

The novel is set in a fictional town called Barrytown, just north of Dublin in Ireland. The year is 1968.

Barrytown is supposedly a new suburb, created in the countryside just beyond Dublin. Although the novel mostly focuses on Paddy's own family and the small community around them, Paddy does make reference to national and world events even when he does not always understand them.

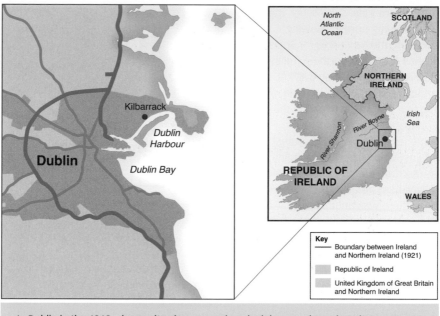

In Dublin in the 1960s, inner-city slums were knocked down and new housing estates spread out across the surrounding countryside, eventually becoming suburbs

It is relevant to note that Roddy Doyle and his **protagonist** were born in the same year, and Barrytown may be based on Doyle's childhood home of Kilbarrack. As such, we might assume that some of the novel is **autobiographical**.

> **autobiographical writing** the story of a person's life written by him or herself
>
> **protagonist** the central character in a novel

Ireland and Northern Ireland

Although the novel is set in the late 1960s, the partition (splitting in two) of Ireland in 1921 was a relatively recent event in the characters' histories. Partition meant that the southern part of Ireland became the Irish Free Republic (now the Republic of Ireland), whereas Northern Ireland remained part of the UK. Paddy's father, for example, would have been born in the early 1930s, just over a decade after the split, and the influence of it in all their lives would have been significant. In fact, when Paddy talks to his father of his worries about World War Three, they end up discussing the State's separation from the UK and, in response to Paddy's comment **'We won'**, his father replies, **'Yes. We murdered them. We gave them a hiding they'll never forget'** (page 30).

It appears that Paddy and his father see independence from the UK in heroic terms. This is reinforced by the description of Miss Watkins, the teacher before Mister Hennessey, who makes all the boys march and clap in honour of the seven men who signed the Proclamation of Independence in 1916.

In Northern Ireland, however, there was growing unrest following partition: the Campaign for Social Justice (CSJ), the Northern Ireland Civil Rights Association (NICRA) and several other groups held the first civil rights march in the country in early 1968. These marches were staged to protest against what was seen by many as discrimination against Catholics in Northern Ireland. Later that year, there was another Civil Rights March in Derry, organized by members of the Derry Housing Action Committee (DHAC) and

British troops seal off Dublin streets after the Proclamation of Independence in 1916

supported by NICRA. It was stopped by the Royal Ulster Constabulary (RUC) who broke up the march by force; many people were injured, including a number of members of Parliament (MPs). Because of the media presence at the march, it was filmed and the coverage was shown worldwide. There followed two days of rioting by residents of Derry. These events are often identified as the beginning of the 'Troubles' in Northern Ireland, a period of violence that lasted until the late 1990s.

Activity 1

What do you think Paddy's father means in the following passage?

Key quotations

'... the people in the shops were friends with our parents. They'd all got married and moved to Barrytown at the same time. They were all pioneers, my da said. I didn't know what he meant but he liked saying it.' *(page 157)*

World events

A number of significant events took place in 1968:

- the Palestine Liberation Organization (PLO) appointed a new leader, Yasir Arafat
- the USA was at war with Vietnam
- Martin Luther King Jr was shot in April
- the Soviet Union invaded Czechoslovakia in August
- Apollo 7 was launched in October, followed by Apollo 8 in December
- the Olympic Games took place in Mexico City in October.

Activity 2

On pages 24–30, Paddy talks to his father about world events, following on from his anxiety about a newspaper front page article headlined 'World War Three Looms Near'.

a) Make a list of all the subjects that come from this initial topic of conversation. If you wish, you can present your list as a mind map or flow chart to show all the diversions that the conversation takes.

b) Create a table with two columns. In one column, make a list of all the questions that Paddy asks his father and, in the other, make a list of all the questions his father asks him. What do you notice about their questions? What differences are there?

c) How do you think Paddy feels about the headline, and the possible conflict, after the conversation with his father? Do you think he is still worrying about it or has he forgotten it? Why do you think Paddy finishes the section by mentioning what they had for dinner?

Religion

Paddy's family is Catholic and Catholicism clearly has a major influence on his life and upbringing. Religious stories, traditions and events permeate the everyday lives of the Barrytown community; for example:

- Paddy comments that it is his job to do the dusting before the family go to mass on Sunday mornings.
- He describes the picture of Jesus in his parents' bedroom with the children's names and dates of birth written in.
- He refers to the story of Father Damien and the lepers.
- He makes his own hosts (Communion wafers) from Vienna roll and Batch bread.
- Paddy announces to his parents that he has a vocation and is going to be a missionary.
- He talks about Sinbad's Holy Communion.
- Father Moloney visits the school every month.
- Paddy contemplates the nature of sin.
- Paddy refers to Alan Baxter, the only boy in Barrytown with Scalextric, as 'a **Protestant, a proddy**' *(page 113)*.
- His father jokes about the Bible, for example, '**Where was Moses when the lights went out?**' *(page 145)*.
- Paddy prays when his parents are fighting.
- He relates events at Keith Simpson's funeral.

27

Activity 3

Compare Paddy's parents' reactions to his announcement that he is going to become a missionary *(pages 52–53)* and their comments when he asks about wearing jeans on a Sunday *(page 61)*. What does this show us about their attitudes to religion? What evidence is there that Doyle is trying to show us changing perceptions of religion in Ireland in the late 1960s?

Popular culture

The television and newspaper are both central to Paddy's father's identity and the ways in which Paddy understands him. Throughout the novel he often judges his father's mood by whether he is reading the newspaper or just rustling it, whether he is pretending to read the newspaper but really watching the television or whether he is viewing a programme on television with interest.

The television would have been a black and white set and would have had a limited number of channels: RTÉ Television (the only Irish channel, launched in 1961), BBC Northern Ireland and possibly an ITV channel. Programmes and films that Paddy mentions are *Voyage to the Bottom of the Sea*, *The Fugitive* and an unnamed cowboy film that his father is watching one evening.

Paddy also makes reference to his mother listening to the radio show *The Kennedys of Castleross*, a lunchtime soap opera that ran from 1955 to 1975 on Radio Éireann.

Football is a big part of Paddy's life and he is particularly entranced by George Best and his football skills. He refers to watching the European Cup Final on television and is so overjoyed at Best's goal for Manchester United that he runs around the garden because **'The house wasn't big enough'** *(page 133).*

As well as reading the newspaper, his father reads a book called *The Naked and the Dead*, written by Norman Mailer. It tells the story of a US infantry platoon stationed on a Japanese-held island in the south Pacific during the Second World War. Paddy's mother also reads books, but the titles remain unknown to us; Paddy merely reports that he always counts up how many pages she has read.

This scene from the film *The Commitments*, based on another of Doyle's novels set in Barrytown, demonstrates the juxtaposition of religion and popular culture in the lives of the inhabitants

Northern Irish football player, George Best, here playing for Manchester United in 1968, was a hero to many small boys

Marriage, divorce and children

One of the central themes of the novel is the breakdown of Paddy's parents' marriage. Divorce in Ireland was not legal until 1996 despite, as Paddy muses, there being large numbers of separated couples.

> **Key quotations**
>
> **Mister O'Driscoll from the house at the top of the old road didn't live there any more. He wasn't dead either; I'd seen him. Richard Shiels's da sometimes didn't live in their house. […] Edward Swanwick's ma ran away with a pilot from Aer Lingus. […] She never came back. […] We were next. I knew it, and I was going to be ready.** *(page 245)*

Paddy is one of five children, although a sister, Angela, was stillborn. As Catholics, his parents would have been taught that sexual intercourse should only take place for the purpose of procreation and for many years it was illegal to sell contraceptives in Ireland or for them to be imported into the country.

Paddy describes the picture of Jesus in his parents' bedroom with their wedding date and the names of all of their children: **'There was room for six more names'** *(page 38).*

> **Activity 4**
>
> Near the end of the novel, Paddy reports the taunting chant that he hears:
>
> '   Paddy Clarke –
>
> Paddy Clarke –
>
> Has no da.
>
> Ha ha ha!' *(page 281)*
>
> What does this suggest to you about people's attitudes and, in particular, a child's understanding towards marriage breakdown at the time?

Housing and lifestyle

The countryside around Paddy's home disappears through the novel as new estates of 'Corporation houses' are erected. In 1963, Dubliners marched through the streets of the city to protest about the state of the slums after two ten-year-old girls and a husband and wife were killed in separate instances by houses that literally fell down on top of them. In response, new estates were built on the outskirts of the city and many people from the inner-city slums were rehoused there. Although the novel's setting is fictional, we can probably assume that the housing referred to is based on the new estates being created at the time.

We see differing attitudes to these new arrivals when Paddy refers to the children from the Corporation houses in a derogatory manner and his mother reacts by hitting him.

> **Key quotations**
>
> — Slum scum.
>
> My ma hit me when I said that. She never hit me usually but she did then. She smacked behind my head.
>
> — Never say that again.
>
> — I didn't make it up, I told her.
>
> — Just never say it again, she said. — It's a terrible thing to say.
>
> I didn't even know what it really meant. I knew that the slums were in town. *(page 118)*

New housing estates were built on the outskirts of Dublin in the 1960s

We can tell by Paddy's mother's reaction to his language that she has never said it, so he must have heard it outside the confines of his home. This, and Paddy's general hostility towards the children in the Corporation houses, suggests that some of his friends must have learned this attitude from their parents and siblings.

Paddy's parents are presented to us as aspirational and relatively financially secure. Paddy never reports any discussion about money or makes mention of any hardship in the home.

- Paddy's mother does not go out to work and mothers who do are obviously rare because Paddy recalls a conversation with his mother about it: 'My ma said that Missis McEvoy only worked in Cadbury's because she had to' *(page 34)*.
- His parents buy a Ford Cortina and his father teaches himself to drive.
- His father brings home a record player and they have three records.

Activity 5

a) What does the key quotation on page 31 show us about Paddy's mother?

b) Why do you think Doyle includes this passage, and the conversation between Paddy and his mother that follows it, in the novel?

Key quotations

The front room was not for going into. It was the drawing room. Nobody else had a drawing room although all the houses were the same, all the houses before the Corporation ones. Our drawing room was Kevin's ma's and da's living room, and Ian McEvoy's television room. Ours was the drawing room because my ma said it was. *(page 137)*

Writing about context

Upgrade

The information in this chapter will help you to understand the text and write about the novel and the writer's purpose more convincingly. However, beware of 'bolting on' historical information or including irrelevant facts in your answers. It does not really tell the examiner anything useful if you write, 'Roddy Doyle was born in 1958. Paddy Clarke is ten in the novel.' However, if there is a link between the two, then it can be relevant to your answer. For example:

> Roddy Doyle was born in 1958; this is the same year that his protagonist, Paddy, was born. Barrytown, the fictional town of Paddy's childhood, is also in a similar location to Doyle's real childhood home of Kilbarrack. Many of Paddy's experiences, therefore, are likely to be similar to, or adaptations of, Doyle's own childhood events, understanding or games.

There is no need to write a historical essay about world events or social attitudes in 1968, but you can highlight that Paddy's fears when he does not fully understand the newspaper headline were probably experienced by many children at that time. Similarly, the anguish Paddy suffers over the breakdown of his parents' marriage is not only because it is a horrible situation, but also because divorce was not legal in Ireland until the mid-1990s.

Characters

The characters in *Paddy Clarke Ha Ha Ha* can be separated into four fairly distinct groups around the central character of Paddy: his family; his friends and classmates; adults at school; and other minor characters.

Paddy

Paddy is the narrator of the novel and its **eponymous** protagonist. Aged ten, he lives in Barrytown with his parents, his younger brother Francis (nicknamed Sinbad) and his sisters, Catherine and Deirdre.

The novel is told in the first person, from Paddy's perspective. Although he has a number of friends, he is always insecure and anxious about his friendship with Kevin and where he is in the **hierarchy** of Kevin's friendships. At the beginning of the novel, Paddy tells us that he once put his finger on the bar of a heater 'because Kevin told me to' *(page 44)*.

> **eponymous** the person after whom something is named
>
> **hierarchy** a system that ranks people or groups according to status
>
> **irony** the discrepancy between what a character could be expected to do and what they actually do, often for comic effect

> **Key quotations**
>
> We were lying in the long grass […] I knew the answer but I didn't say it. Kevin knew the answer; that was why he'd asked the question. I knew that. I could tell by his voice. I never answered Kevin's questions. I never rushed with an answer, in school or anywhere; I always gave him a chance to answer first. *(page 46)*

Although Paddy does not understand a lot of what he reports, we get a sense of his growing awareness of the inequality of his friendship with Kevin.

Near the end of the novel, Paddy, although still a child, realizes that Kevin's behaviour is often cruel and thoughtless and that he is fickle in his friendships. Paddy's comments reflect his growing awareness of what has happened.

> **Key quotations**
>
> No one had jumped in for me when Charles Leavy had been going to kill me; it took me a while to get used to that, to make it make sense. To make it alright. The quiet, the waiting. All of them looking. Kevin standing beside Seán Whelan. Looking. *(pages 186–187)*

Paddy is, **ironically**, very honest to the reader about the fibs he tells to Kevin, which include:

- his Grandad Clarke is the Thomas Clarke who signed the Irish Proclamation of Independence
- the drowned boy, Keith Simpson, was his cousin
- he has an aunt who called the guards (Irish police) after his uncle hit her.

> **Key quotations**
>
> I loved making up stuff; I loved the way the next bit came into my head, it made sense and expanded and I could keep going till I came to the end; it was like being in a race. I always won. *(page 229)*

Paddy makes frequent references to family mealtimes throughout the novel. When narrating his first adventure, he comments, 'We were going home for our dinner; shepherd's pie on a Tuesday' *(page 3)*, which reflects the regular timetable of family meals together. Later, after spending time chatting to his father about the possibility of another world war, he reflects, 'We had our dinner. It was lovely. The mince wasn't too runny' *(page 30)*. When his parents' marriage is disintegrating, however, there is an episode in which his mother does not clear the dinner table before breakfast the next morning and he is bewildered and angry by the mess left on the table.

The abandoned dishes on the dinner table reflects the disintegration of order in Paddy's family life

> **Key quotations**
>
> It was stupid, not doing the dishes in the night. The food was still soft then and easy to get off; it came off in the water. Now, though, she was going to have to rub real hard. Loads of elbow grease. Blood, sweat and tears. She'd have her work cut out for her. It served her right. She should have done them the night before; that was the proper time to do them. *(page 176)*

Key quotations

— Why did you not do the dishes?

Something happened when I was asking it; it was in my voice, a difference between the beginning and the end. The reason – it fell into me. The reason she hadn't done the dishes. I'd been in a lift once – twice – up, then down. This was like going down. I nearly didn't finish: I knew the answer. It unwrapped while I was talking. The reason. *(page 178)*

This is a very vivid example of Paddy recognizing, as he asks the question, what the truth of the situation is. The short sentences and the **analogy** of the lift show how stunned he is when he realizes what has happened; his anger turns to shock at the enormity of the event. The dinner table is the centre of the family's life together and Paddy suddenly sees what is happening to it.

analogy a comparison which highlights similarities

Activity 1

1. Paddy's age is reflected in the way that he narrates the novel. At the opening of the book, we see Paddy coming home from an outing with his friends and brother. Make a list of everything that we learn from this first page of Paddy's narrative.

2. Continue to annotate the following piece of text to show Paddy's understanding of how friendship with Kevin works.

> Friendship with Kevin is everything. This word makes not being a friend sound as if there is nothing else.
>
> Liam was finished now; Kevin and me wouldn't even talk to him any more. I was delighted. I didn't know why. I liked Liam. It seemed important though. If you were going to be best friends with anyone – Kevin – you had to hate a lot of other people, the two of you, together. It made you better friends. And now Liam was sitting beside Charles Leavy. There was just me and Kevin now, no one else. *(pages 181–182)*
>
> They will completely ignore Liam so he will be isolated.
>
> He's very happy at the thought of someone else's misfortune.

3. **a)** What do you notice about the lies Paddy tells Kevin?

   b) Why do you think Paddy enjoys lying so much?

4. As you read the novel, take note of comments made about food, eating, the dinner table and family mealtimes. This will help you chart the decline of Paddy's family and the way in which the dinner table becomes an image of the family's fortunes.

Paddy's family

Da

Paddy's father is a figure of contrasts: at one moment kind and interested, and the next cruel and bullying. Paddy's father is presented as a figure of authority and fear from the moment he is first mentioned, when his mother discovers that Paddy has been setting fires.

Key quotations

She killed me. The worst part was waiting to see if she'd tell my da when he came home. *(page 6)*

Despite this introduction, Paddy's father initially also seems to be loving, interested and funny. Paddy describes his father explaining to him that everyone's fingerprints are different and showing him how to look at them through a magnifying glass.

His hands are discussed again when Paddy describes them in detail.

Paddy's feelings about his father can be understood from his descriptions of Da's hands at key moments in the novel

Key quotations

My da's hands were big. The fingers were long. They weren't fat. I could make out the bone under the skin and the flesh. [...] His nails were clean – except for one – and the white bits at the top were longer than mine. The wrinkles at his knuckles were a bit like the design of a wall, the cement between the bricks up and across. *(page 24)*

As the story unfolds, Paddy's parents argue more and more, and then Paddy hears his father hit his mother. At the end of the text, Paddy's father has left the family home but he returns to visit on Christmas Eve and shakes Paddy's hand: **'His hand felt cold and big, dry and hard'** *(page 282)*.

Through the novel Paddy's father becomes increasingly sullen and temperamental towards all his family. However, Paddy does recall times when his father was cheerful and the family enjoyed his company. Near the beginning of the book, his parents laugh together about his mother mistakenly thinking Uncle Eddie was dead and about the Swanwicks always having **'Nothing but the best'** *(page 16)*. Paddy also recalls a time when his father put a blanket over him when he fell asleep under the dining room table. However, his father's attitude has changed and so Paddy claims that he can't do it now as **'I was afraid I'd be caught'** *(page 104)*.

Paddy presents his father as a man who was once happy but who has always had a volatile temper, and Paddy is constantly anxious about displeasing him. When his father is learning to drive the car, he won't let Paddy and his friends ride with him, although they follow him to the seafront anyway.

Paddy's father often reads books, newspapers and watches television, particularly the news. At the beginning of the novel, Paddy is able to ask him about a newspaper headline and about the book he is reading, but both the reading and the television watching become **symbols** of his father's increasing misery and the tensions within the household.

symbolism using something to represent a concept, idea or theme in a novel

Key quotations

He was good sometimes and useless others and sometimes you could tell that you couldn't go near him to ask him or tell him anything. He didn't like being distracted; he said that word a lot, but I knew what it meant, Distracted, and I didn't know how he was being distracted because he wasn't doing anything anyway. [...] He had to get his energy back at the weekend. Sometimes I didn't believe that that was the only reason for not being able to go near him, for the way he got into his corner and wouldn't come out. Sometimes he was just being mean. *(pages 202–203)*

As we read the novel, we need to remember that Paddy's narrative is that of a child; he sees everything from his ten-year-old viewpoint and therefore a lot of what he tells us can be inconsistent. He tries to make sense of his father's behaviour and sometimes accepts it because he knows no different.

Activity 2

1. Look at Paddy's descriptions of his father's hands on page 24 and at the very end of the novel.

    a) What does the description of Paddy's father's hands on page 24 show us about Paddy's relationship with his father at this point in the novel?

    b) What does the gesture of shaking hands at the end of the novel and Paddy's description tell us about the father and son relationship now?

    c) Why do you think Doyle has this meeting, and gesture, as the final moments of the novel?

    d) What other moments are there where Paddy's father touches him or Sinbad? How does Paddy feel about them?

2. Look at the four quotations below and explain what they show us:

    • about Paddy's father

    • about what Paddy thinks is important

    • about Paddy's growing awareness of his parents' failing marriage.

Key quotations

A year after that I knew that it wasn't George Best's real autograph at all; it was only printing and my da was a liar. *(page 137)*

Fathers were like that, all the fathers I knew... *(page 203)*

I sometimes didn't believe it; I'd really think that there was nothing wrong – the way they were chatting and drinking their tea, the way we all looked at the television – but I'd swing back again before happiness could trap me. She was lovely. He was nice. *(page 244)*

My da had more wrong with him than my ma. [...] My da sometimes lost his temper and he liked it. [...] He was useless at lots of things. He never finished games. He read the newspapers. He coughed. He sat too much. *(page 258)*

Ma

Paddy's mother, or Ma, is presented as a much gentler character than his father – someone who has aspirations, is a victim of her husband's tempestuous moods, fair in her disciplining of the children and non-judgemental towards others.

She reads and knits in the evenings. She does not consider herself particularly at ease with world affairs, telling Paddy to ask his father about the Second World War. However, she has aspirations: she refers to their reception room as the 'drawing room', something that Paddy finds difficult to understand; tells Paddy that she does not have to go out to work because his father has a **'better job than Ian's daddy'** *(page 34)*; and smacks Paddy for referring to the children in the Corporation houses as **'Slum scum'** *(page 118)*.

The first time Paddy's mother is mentioned is when Paddy recalls telling her that Kevin told him about Liam and Aidan's father howling at the moon: **'My ma said that he did it because he missed his wife'** *(page 3)*. She does not comment on the tale told by Kevin or tell Paddy it's a ridiculous story; she merely acknowledges the man's grief. She is, from the outset, seen as a kindly and gentle presence in Paddy's life – someone that Paddy goes to for sympathy and kindness before going to his father, who is so much more unpredictable in his responses.

Key quotations

She didn't lose her temper. *(page 31)*

Her voice hadn't changed; she wasn't going to bully him. *(page 32)*

She always stopped and listened. *(page 164)*

Paddy's mother tries to be the mediator between her husband and children when she realizes her husband is getting angry: **'Don't shout at him, Paddy, my ma said to my da, not to us; we weren't supposed to hear it'** *(page 37)*. She does administer corporal punishment to her children, but Paddy explains it as if her response is more predictable and reasonable than his father's. When Sinbad loses his shoe at the building site and then lies to say that he does not remember where he left it, their mother smacks the back of his legs. Although she does physically punish them for bad behaviour, Paddy also tells us on a number of occasions that his mother nearly cried when she hit them.

Paddy's mother is much more tender towards her children than her husband is. When Paddy thinks he has been stung by a jellyfish, she asks him if she should go next door and telephone for an ambulance.

At the beginning of the novel, she appears to be secure in her relationship with her husband. Paddy tells us that when there is the misunderstanding over Uncle Eddie's death between his parents: **'There was a gap and then they burst out laughing, the two of them'** *(page 14)*. Although only one sentence, it tells us a lot about the happiness of Paddy's parents: they are a unit, enjoying a joke between themselves.

Although Paddy appears to narrate events as he sees them and is, in many ways, as immature at the end of the novel as he is at the beginning, we can see his implicit understanding of his father's bullying of his mother and the ways in which she is being worn down. He recognizes that his mother is lonely and desperate to keep her family together despite not understanding her reasons.

Key quotations

I didn't understand. She was lovely. He was nice. They had four children [...] She held onto us for longer, gripped us and looked over us at the floor or the ceiling. [...] But she wasn't cuddling us; she was hanging on to us. *(page 222)*

Paddy's parents are very separate to Paddy's friends, inhabiting different worlds in the novel. Paddy comments that his mother and Kevin's mother **'didn't like each other much; you could tell from the way they kept moving when they met each other on the street or outside the shops, like they were too busy to stop for long, they were in a hurry'** *(page 230)*. At the close of the novel, Paddy's mother seems completely isolated and friendless: when his father returns for a visit, **'Ma stayed in the kitchen; she was busy'** *(page 281)*.

Activity 3

Read the passage from 'I have a vocation, I said' to 'They didn't say anything' *(pages 52–53)*. Copy and complete the spider diagram below to illustrate all that you learn about Paddy's mother from the passage.

Paddy's mother

Takes an interest: 'Has someone been talking to you?' (page 52)

Considers what she's been told: 'She looked like she was making her mind up.' (page 53)

Sinbad (Francis)

Sinbad (real name, Francis) is Paddy's younger brother, who bears, through most of the novel, the brunt of Paddy's torments. At the beginning he is out with Paddy and his friends on the building site but when his sleeve becomes caught on a thorny hedge Paddy writes, **'We left Sinbad stuck in the hedge and pretended we'd run away. We heard him snivelling'** *(page 3)*. Paddy appears to take pleasure in tormenting Sinbad and taunting him to make himself seem more impressive in front of his friends. He feels that, as the older brother, he should be able to control Sinbad. When Sinbad refuses to put the lighter fuel in his mouth, Paddy states, **'This was terrible; in front of the others I couldn't sort out my little brother'** *(page 8)*.

Sinbad is depicted as a serious, quiet, inward child, who remains seemingly unaffected by much of the torment he suffers. When Kevin gives him a Chinese burn, **'he didn't seem to notice the pain, so Kevin stopped'** *(page 161)*. In some ways, he is presented as the **stereotypical** younger sibling; Paddy thinks he 'gets away' with much more than he can himself and, if Sinbad cries, his parents comfort him or stop the punishment he is being given. When he is being smacked across the back of the legs for losing his shoe, he manages to keep ahead of his mother so she cannot hit him accurately: **'He still cried though, and she stopped'** *(page 4)*.

> **stereotype** a common but overly simplified view of a particular type of person

Paddy also suggests to us that if it is evident someone has done something wrong in their family, it is assumed that he was the culprit and he will get the blame rather than Sinbad. At mass, when Sinbad laughs at Uncle Eddie, Paddy **'looked at my da to make sure that he didn't think it was me'** *(page 12)* and when his mother sees the boys stealing from the shops at Raheny, Paddy thinks, **'She'd be waiting behind the wall, waiting. She'd smack me, and give me Sinbad's share as well, in front of the others'** *(page 161)*. There are occasions when Sinbad unintentionally breaks the tension between his father and the rest of the family, for example, when he tells his Da they could get a dog with no hair and his father laughs: **'He thought it was a great joke'** *(page 145)*. Paddy is bewildered by what he sees and later in the novel he states, **'He could stop everything happening, and I couldn't'** *(page 240)*.

Despite his negative feelings about Sinbad, Paddy does, often secretly, help him out. When, for example, their father threatens to punish Sinbad if he does not finish his dinner, Paddy comments, **'I helped Sinbad eat his dinner. [...] He made Sinbad sit there for an hour until he was ready to inspect the plate. It was nearly empty; in me and in the bin'** *(page 37)*.

Sinbad is seen as a victim by many other characters in the novel: he was tormented by Kevin's older brother and friends when they painted the clear lens of his glasses black and made him walk home with a white stick. Their mother comforts him, but did nothing about it. Again, we see Paddy's ambivalence in that he offers to help Sinbad clean the black paint off his glasses but then laughs about the incident with his father.

As their father's angry outbursts escalate, Paddy becomes increasingly protective of Sinbad. Paddy suggests to us that Sinbad does not understand their parents' rows in the way that he does.

> **Key quotations**
>
> Sinbad didn't notice the way I did. There had to be shouts and screams and big gaps between them before he knew anything. When it was quiet it was fine; that was the way he thought. He wouldn't agree with me, even when I got him on the ground. *(page 153)*
>
> It's only talking, he said. *(page 223)*

Through the narrative, Paddy begins to recognize that Sinbad is more than **'just my little brother'** *(page 167)* and becomes increasingly impressed by him, although he often does not admit it. Initially he confesses that he only realizes that Sinbad is good at football because Mister O'Keefe tells him he is, but later on he is in awe of Sinbad's calm manner: **'I could kill him in fights but the way he went scared me. He let me give him a hiding and then he just went away'** *(page 189)*.

Sinbad is often depicted as an isolated figure, on the outside of Paddy's friendship group

As Paddy loses his friends, he looks to Sinbad more often for sympathetic company, although he still tries to hide his true feelings and he is horrified when he thinks his brother might have realized the truth.

> **Key quotations**
>
> He'd found out; he'd found out. I'd wanted him to talk because I was scared. Pretending to be protecting him, I'd wanted him close to me, to share, to listen together; to stop it or run away. He knew: I was frightened and lonely, more than he was. *(page 260)*

Activity 4

1. Read the passage from 'I knew what Paddy meant ...' to 'Yeah, said Sinbad' (pages 126–127).

   a) Paddy writes that he knows why Sinbad 'laughed, and made himself laugh more'. Why do you think he does it?

   b) Why does their Da ask so many questions at the beginning of the conversation?

   c) What does Paddy think he has saved Sinbad from?

   d) What evidence is there in the extract that Sinbad realizes that Paddy is protecting him?

   e) What, if any, changes do you notice in Sinbad through this extract?

2. Throughout most of the novel, Paddy refers to Francis as Sinbad, but near the end of the novel Paddy explains:

> **Key quotations**
>
> **I thought of something.**
>
> **— Do you not like being called Sinbad?**
>
> **— No.**
>
> **— Okay.**
>
> **I said nothing for a bit. I heard him change, move nearer the wall.**
>
> **— Francis?** *(pages 222–223)*

   Why do you think Paddy decides to start calling his brother by his real name? What does it suggest about their relationship and how Paddy feels about him?

Angela, Catherine and Deirdre

Paddy has younger sisters. Angela was the next child after Paddy but was stillborn. Catherine and Deirdre are babies in the novel and are only mentioned occasionally: Paddy has to rock Deirdre in the pram; Catherine was a baby and his mother was pregnant with Deirdre when they went on the picnic in the Ford Cortina; his mother was pushing the pram when she saw the boys shoplifting at Raheny; Paddy compares going up stairs with a book on his head to Catherine's first teetering baby steps.

Paddy's friends and classmates

Kevin

Kevin is, for most of the novel, the boy Paddy would really like to be his best friend and he is the leader of all of the games the group of friends play. The way he is introduced to us by Paddy leads us to understand that they are best friends: 'We were coming down our road. [...] Liam and Aidan turned down their cul-de-sac. We said nothing; they said nothing' *(page 1)*. However, we soon learn that Kevin is, in many ways, like Paddy's father – a bully who often behaves cruelly for no apparent reason. It is Kevin who gets Paddy in trouble at school for claiming his grandfather was the Thomas Clarke who signed the Irish Proclamation of Independence.

Through the first part of the novel we can see that Paddy and his classmates believe what Kevin tells them.

Key quotations

Kevin said that they couldn't do anything to you if they didn't catch you on the building site. *(page 6)*

We saw mice. I never saw any, but I heard them. I said I saw them. Kevin saw loads of them. *(page 13)*

However, we realize that Paddy does doubt Kevin's truthfulness but often keeps quiet for fear of spoiling their friendship. When Paddy recalls the story of the burning barn, he says, 'Later, about a year after, Kevin said he'd done it. But he didn't. He was in Courtown in a caravan on his holidays when it happened. I didn't say anything' *(pages 14–15)*. Paddy is often in fear of losing Kevin's friendship or of somebody else taking his place as Kevin's best friend, so he remains silent when he knows Kevin is not being truthful.

Kevin is quite a violent character: he kicks Ian McEvoy's mother's dog; dangles the boy over the side of the garage on the new housing estate; and hits his friends across the back with a poker when they are chanting around the fire.

As the story progresses, Paddy becomes increasingly aware of Kevin's mindless cruelty and his gossipy nature. He regrets trying to talk to Kevin about his parents fighting: 'I shouldn't have asked Kevin in the first place; he was the wrong one. I should have asked Liam. I'd escaped, but Kevin would probably tell his ma now about my uncle and auntie and she'd tell my ma' *(page 230)*.

The boys' friendship seems to build steadily until the moment when the two boys from the Corporation houses arrive. Paddy is thrilled when Charles Leavy is sat next to Liam as he feels this makes his own friendship with Kevin stronger.

Key quotations

If you were going to be best friends with anyone – Kevin – you had to hate a lot of other people, the two of you, together. It made you better friends. *(page 182)*

However, from this moment of realization, Paddy begins to distance himself from Kevin and is almost not bothered by Kevin's reaction – to ostracize (exclude) him from the rest of their friendship group. We can see that Kevin is upset at losing Paddy's friendship to Charles Leavy and Paddy's admission that he's been out smoking in the field '**With Charlo**' *(page 270)* leads Kevin to threaten him. However, Paddy also shows us that Kevin has been isolating Paddy and not helping him when he's in trouble for some time, for example, when Paddy fights with Charles Leavy and Kevin stands at the edge just watching with Seán Whelan.

Activity 5

1. As you read the novel, keep a note of Kevin's behaviour, how Paddy explains it to us and the ways in which Paddy's reaction to it changes. You could use a table like the partially-completed one below.

Point	Evidence	Explanation
Kevin is the leader of the boys' gang.	'Kevin patted me on the back. So did Liam.' (page 7)	Kevin is always the first to act and then the others copy him. They wait until he has decided what to do before they mimic his actions.
Kevin often gets the other boys in trouble despite being involved himself.		
	'I'd done that once, because Kevin told me to, put my finger on the bar of the heater.' (page 44)	
		Although Paddy recognizes that Kevin acts unfairly he rarely says anything for fear of being ostracized from the group.

2. Look at the list below of various events in Paddy and Kevin's friendship. Decide which one of these you think is the most significant. Put the events in order, starting with the most important.

- Paddy knows that Kevin lied about being responsible for the barn burning down.

- Paddy sees the dirty mark in Kevin's pants.

- Kevin pokes Paddy in the eyes like the characters in the film *The Three Stooges*.

- Kevin 'pruned' Paddy after Paddy finds him in the pipe.

- Kevin stands on the edge of the circle, next to Seán Whelan, and watches while Charles Leavy fights Paddy.

- Paddy calls Kevin an offensive name to Charles Leavy.

- Kevin and Paddy fight in the playground.

- Paddy tells Kevin, 'I saw the gick marks on your underpants' *(page 272)*.

- Kevin sends David Geraghty to hit Paddy with one of his crutches.

- Paddy hears a group of children chanting, 'Paddy Clarke – / Paddy Clarke – / Has no da' *(page 281)*.

Charles Leavy

Although Charles only appears in the second half of the novel, he plays a pivotal role in Paddy's friendship with Kevin and in the way Paddy deals with the breakdown of his parents' marriage. When he first appears in Paddy's class, Paddy does not like him because he is from one of the Corporation houses; Kevin says: **'They should be put in the thicks' class'** *(page 180)*. Paddy is thrilled when Charles is sat next to Liam as he sees this as cementing his own position of friendship with Kevin: **'It was great. Liam was finished now; Kevin and me wouldn't even talk to him any more'** *(page 181)*.

From very early on, Paddy is in awe of Charles; he thinks that Charles would be unbeatable in a fight. However, Charles is the only one who does not participate in 'kneeding' or 'boring' anyone when the craze sweeps through school.

When Paddy and Kevin play football with Charles and Seán Whelan, Paddy sees that they have a much more equal friendship than him and Kevin. He is envious of it and wants recognition from Charles and to be his friend. He seeks him out more and more: smoking with him on school grounds one day and following him out at break.

What appeals to Paddy most about Charles is his aloof nature and the fact that he does not care about others' opinions of him; Paddy sees his behaviour as useful protection against hurt when his parents' marriage breaks down.

Key quotations

I wanted to be like Charles Leavy. I wanted to be hard. [...] Charles Leavy didn't dare anyone; he'd gone further than that: he didn't know they were there. I wanted to get that far. I wanted to look at my ma and da and not feel anything. I wanted to be ready. *(page 250)*

Activity 6

Continue to annotate what we learn about Charles from Paddy's description.

The other boys are scared of him.

Charles Leavy wore plastic sandals, blue ones. We laughed at them but we were careful. He brought nothing into school the first day. When Henno asked why not he said nothing, he just looked at his sleeves on the desk. He didn't squirm. There was nearly a hole in one of his elbows. You could see lots of his shirt through it. His hair was very short, the same all over his head. Now and again he stretched his neck and sort of shot his head out to the side, like he was heading a ball but not bothering to look at it. He looked, and I looked away. I felt hot, scared. *(page 184)*

Cheap and the wrong colour for school.

He's not ashamed and not afraid of the teacher.

Other friends and classmates

Liam and **Aidan O'Connell** are brothers and Liam is in Paddy and Kevin's class. Both boys are part of Paddy's friendship group, although there is often animosity between Liam and Paddy due to competition to be Kevin's best friend. Liam and Aidan's mother is dead and so they live with their father, who does all the housework. Paddy describes the two brothers and comments on how similar they are when together, but how different when separate.

Key quotations

When the brothers were together, standing beside each other, it was easy to see them the way we saw them; little, jokes, sad, nice. They were our friends because we hated them; it was good to have them around. I was cleaner than them, brainier than them. I was better than them. Separate, it was different. Aidan got smaller, unfinished looking. Liam became dangerous. They looked the same together. They were nothing alike when you met one of them alone. That nearly never happened. *(page 167)*

Throughout the novel, there are hints that the brothers are ill at ease with the other boys.

Ian McEvoy and **James O'Keefe** are two more members of Paddy's friendship group: they form part of the gang that plays in the fields and building sites and commit petty crimes. James O'Keefe owns the guinea pig that the boys try to steal the sawdust for and it is Ian McEvoy's dog that Kevin kicks.

Seán Whelan starts in Paddy's class at the same time as Charles Leavy and is the other boy from the Corporation homes. Paddy hates him because of where he lives and comments, '**He'd be easy to get. He wouldn't hit back. I'd get him. He wasn't rough looking**' *(page 183)*.

David Geraghty is the boy with polio who often sits alone in class and seems untroubled by his exclusion from the friendship groups around him. At the end of the novel, David is the only boy in the class who actually engages with Paddy when he is 'boycotted'; he is also the symbol of how far Kevin's influence extends when he is sent to kick Paddy in the back with one of his crutches and inform him, '**Kevin said to give you that**' *(page 280)*.

Edward Swanwick is only mentioned in the novel a few times as he goes to a different school, is rarely included in the boys' games and is often singled out for bullying and victimization. It is suggested that his parents are wealthier as he wears a blazer to school and plays rugby.

Other characters

Mister Hennessey

Mister Hennessey is Paddy's teacher. He is depicted as a harsh man who maintains strong discipline in his class, often shouting at and hitting the boys in his charge. He often seems unfair in the way he deals with his pupils: '**He'd be writing something on the board with his back to us and he'd say, — O'Keefe, I know you're up to something down there. Don't let me catch you. He said it one morning and James O'Keefe wasn't even in**' *(pages 1–2)*.

Mister Hennessey does, however, have a more sensitive side to his character. When he catches Paddy fast asleep in class, he carries him out to the Headmaster's study to rest and later calls him back to the room to ask if everything is alright at home.

> **Activity 7**
>
> Read the passage from 'The map was right in my face...' to ' — *Maith thú*' *(pages 234–235)*. Why do you think Doyle includes this episode about Mister Hennessey being kind to Paddy in the novel? What purpose does it serve?

Character map

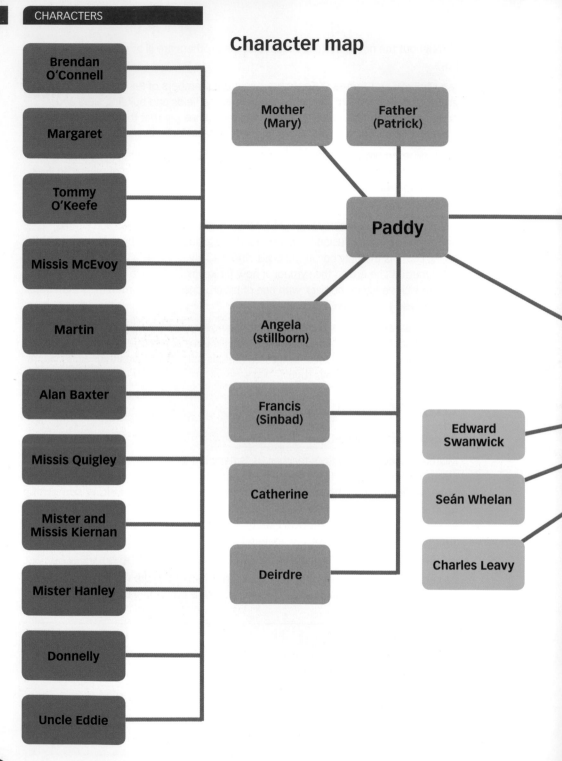

Brendan O'Connell

Margaret

Tommy O'Keefe

Missis McEvoy

Martin

Alan Baxter

Missis Quigley

Mister and Missis Kiernan

Mister Hanley

Donnelly

Uncle Eddie

Mother (Mary)

Father (Patrick)

Paddy

Angela (stillborn)

Francis (Sinbad)

Catherine

Deirdre

Edward Swanwick

Seán Whelan

Charles Leavy

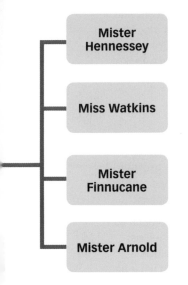

Character map key

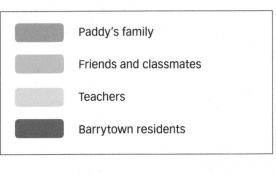

	Paddy's family
	Friends and classmates
	Teachers
	Barrytown residents

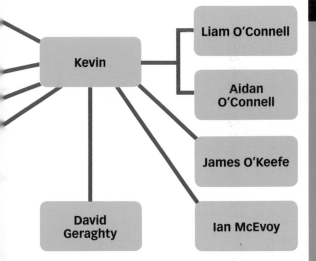

Writing about characters

Upgrade

You need to know about each character in detail and to bear the following in mind:

- An author creates characters for a specific purpose and gives each one particular characteristics and attributes.

- Being able to write fluently about the author's purpose in creating the characters will help you achieve higher marks.

- Being able to comment on the developments in characters will illustrate your understanding of the whole novel.

- Writing expressively about one character and their relationship to another will reflect the cohesion of your understanding.

You always need to use quotations to support the points that you make.

Paddy Clarke Ha Ha Ha is narrated in the first person by Paddy, aged ten years, and, although written in the past tense, he recalls events with immediacy as if they have only just happened. Paddy begins the story without introduction: **'We were coming down our road'** *(page 1)* and we are immediately immersed into his child's view of the world.

Voice and viewpoint

The voice Doyle gives Paddy reflects his age and level of maturity; Paddy uses very simple vocabulary and syntax and includes lots of digressions and **asides** in his speech: **'We were talking about having a dead ma. Sinbad, my little brother, started crying. Liam was in my class at school'** *(page 1).* As readers, we feel as if we are with Paddy, bearing witness to all that he sees and hears as it happens.

The whole story is told by Paddy and from his perspective, although we sometimes gain the opinions of others from Paddy's detailed recollections of conversations, which include other characters' apparently **verbatim** responses. Doyle allows us to understand the views of these characters because Paddy often repeats what he hears without any comment, either positive or negative, so as readers we can **infer** the meaning from the remark.

> **aside** a comment that is not directly relevant to the main topic of discussion
>
> **infer** to guess something based on evidence
>
> **verbatim** reported word for word

Activity 1

Look at this episode that Paddy repeats about Aidan and Liam's father:

> **Key quotations**
>
> Kevin's father said that Mister O'Connell <u>howled because he was drunk</u>. He never called him Mister O'Connell; he called him <u>the Tinker</u>.
>
> — Will you look who's talking, said my mother when I told her that. *(page 3)*

a) What is Kevin's father's opinion of Mister O'Connell? Concentrate on the underlined words to help you answer the question.

b) How does Paddy's mother respond to this information? Consider the tone of her reply and what it is that she comments on: is it the information itself or the source of the information? What does this suggest about her opinion of Kevin's father?

Register and audience

Although we are the 'audience' to all of Paddy's musings in the novel, Doyle illustrates the different situations Paddy finds himself in by altering his **register**. Paddy uses formal, Standard English at times and slang, **colloquial language** and obscenities at others.

While with his friends on the building site, Paddy realizes he's forgotten his jumper and shouts, 'Oh janey. [...] — Emergency, emergency' *(page 6)*, but when he thinks about trying to convince his parents he did not steal the magazines from the shops at Raheny, he imagines himself saying, 'We hadn't been running away, we'd only been running – having a chase' *(page 161)*. The way he speaks to his parents is much more formal, in full sentences, and he wants to imply that there was no sense of panic or crime in what they were doing.

> **colloquial language** informal, everyday speech
>
> **register** a variety of language used in a particular setting; the degree of language formality

Paddy's register in class is polite and formal

At school, Paddy's register and tone changes again. We are witness to his conversation with Mister Hennessey after falling asleep in class, in which he only speaks when spoken to, merely answers the question posed, and always refers to Mister Hennessey as 'Sir'.

> **Key quotations**
>
> — You fell asleep.
>
> — Yes, Sir.
>
> — In class.
>
> — Yes, Sir. I don't remember.
>
> — Did you sleep properly last night?
>
> — Yes, Sir. I woke up early.
>
> — Early.
>
> — Yes, Sir. I heard the cock crow.
>
> — That's early.
>
> — Yes, Sir. *(page 236)*

The short phrases, each one mirroring the one before, suggest that Mister Hennessey does not really know what to say to Paddy; he is unable to communicate with him empathetically and can only repeat what he has just been told in order to continue the conversation.

Throughout the novel Paddy interchanges 'Ma' and 'mother', 'Da' and 'father' when referring to his parents and perhaps we can assume that this is usually Doyle's way of avoiding repetition. When Paddy reports conversations with them, he uses the informal 'Da' and 'Ma'. However, it is telling that at the close of the novel, after Paddy's father has left, he becomes merely the personal pronoun 'he'; his father has lost all personality and meaning to him and has effectively disappeared from Paddy's life.

When answering an extract-based question, remember to focus your answer closely on the passage provided.

Activity 2

Can you think of other examples where Paddy uses different registers?

a) Use a table like the one below to record the quotations and who Paddy is speaking to.

b) Why do you think Doyle shows Paddy speaking in these different ways? What is his purpose in doing so?

Informal, colloquial language, sometimes with obscenities	More Standard English but comfortable conversation	Very formal, short sentences, often only as answers to questions	Formal Standard English, as if reciting from memory or a book
'He did a jobby, I told them all. — Down his leg.' (page 200) (to his friends, about Sinbad)	'Are you still sick? [...] — Do you want me to go to the shops? [...] — We had crisp sandwiches for our lunch, I told her.' (page 218) (when Paddy comes home from school after his mother didn't get up in the morning)	'Nice day out, he said. — Have your breakfast? — Yes, I said. — Francis as well? — Yes.' (page 215) (in response to his father when his mother doesn't get out of bed)	'The real name for soccer was association football. Association football was played with a round ball on a rectangular pitch...' (page 53) (Paddy has learned the rules of football from a book)

Songs, chants, dancing and marching

Throughout the novel there are many songs and chants: the popular songs his father teaches him; the chants that come from Paddy's church-going upbringing; the traditional folk songs he sings to his extended family; and the rude ones all the boys shout out behind people's backs. They offer us flashes of background information to Paddy's life. Even the title of the novel takes its name from the end chant of the novel when Paddy has lost Kevin's friendship.

Activity 3

Keep a record of all the songs, chants, dancing and marching that takes place in the novel so that you can come back to this information later and consider its significance in the text.

English and Irish language

Although the novel is written in English and the characters all appear to speak English in their day-to-day conversations, Irish words and phrases are sprinkled throughout the text. Irish is most notably used in the recollections about school, with Paddy's teachers – first Miss Watkins and then Mister Hennessey – switching back and forth between the two. Miss Watkins says, *'Nach bhfuil sé go h'álainn, lads?'* *(page 20)* as the boys walk past her to see the tea towel with the Irish Proclamation of Independence on it and later when the school watch films Mr Hennessey says, **'Bring your copies with you. *Seasaígí suas'** *(page 68)*. This mixing of the two languages reflects the traditional and formal nature of the school environment, as well as highlighting that the Republic of Ireland is a separate country from the UK, with a different language and cultural heritage.

Characters in the book also use Irish **colloquialisms**. For example, Paddy's father tells him to **'Sit down, you bloody eejit'** *(page 92)* in the car on the way to the picnic. These give the reader more of a sense of the time and place in which the novel is set and help us gain an understanding of the way in which Paddy and the other characters speak.

> **colloquialism** a word or phrase that is informal or non-standard and often characteristic of a particular region or country

Paddy's mother is one of the few characters who never speaks in this way and always uses Standard English. Paddy even gauges the possibility of a row on the basis of whether his mother refers to the television as the 'telly'.

Key quotations

There was nothing wrong. She'd never have said that if there had been. Ma hated half-words and bits of words and words that weren't real ones. Only full, proper words. *(page 209)*

Unfamiliar words and phrases

Throughout the novel, a number of words, phrases and references are used that are unfamiliar to Paddy and, possibly, to the reader. Paddy's father makes the joke, **'Where was Moses when the lights went out?'** *(page 145)*, which Paddy answers even though he does not understand. Da also tells the boys when they ask if it's morning, **'Morning not to get up'** *(page 152)*. Even Paddy's mother, when she realizes Paddy has been setting fires, exclaims with an apparently nonsensical comment, **'Look at your hands, she said. — Your fingernails! My God, Patrick, you must be in mourning for the cat'** *(page 5)*.

These phrases serve to remind us how bewildering Paddy's life is sometimes; there are riddles that make no sense and reflect how confusing, and often humiliating, growing up can be.

Paddy doesn't realize that the Americans were fighting guerrillas, not gorillas, in the Vietnam War 1968

Key quotations

— Why are the yankees fighting the gorillas?

— D'you hear this, Mary? Patrick wants to know why the yanks are fighting gorillas.

They didn't laugh but it was funny, I could tell. I wanted to cry; I'd given something away. I was stupid. I hated being caught, more than anything. I hated it. *(page 227)*

Writing about language

Upgrade

In your exam, you may be asked to show that you understand the language Doyle has used and why he has chosen to use it in the way he has.

Even if language is not formally assessed in your question, you will need to show that you understand how the author has used language to develop his themes and ideas. Questions with 'How…' in them mean that you need to think and write about the methods the writer has used to put across his ideas to the reader. One of the ways is through the language that he has chosen.

Where appropriate, try to pick out specific words and phrases and explore them in detail in relation to the question.

The themes of a novel are ideas that run through it which you can see, explicitly or implicitly, in a variety of situations or events in the text. Lots of themes overlap; see them as connected so you can make fluent links between them in your writing.

Childhood

This theme is central to the novel because, although Paddy is the same age throughout the novel, we see that he grows up and loses his childish innocence as he watches his parents' marriage break down. In this sense, the book could be considered a **coming-of-age novel**.

> **coming-of-age novel** a literary genre focused on the main character's psychological and moral growth

The story opens with Paddy retelling his journey home from playing on the building site and we are immediately immersed into his childish world: 'Quigley Quigley Quigley!' *(page 1)* the children cry as they stop to bash Missis Quigley's gate with a stick before continuing down the road.

Throughout the novel, Paddy continues to tell us of similar incidents such as setting fires, playing football in the road and building dens in the diminishing countryside around his home. However, he is also on a journey into adolescence and adulthood, and this is reflected in the changing way he writes about his games and experiences.

The novel charts Paddy's emotional development, from a carefree, mischievous boy to a thoughtful adolescent

Paddy's emotional journey away from the innocence of his childhood is mirrored by the decreasing space of his gang's territory, which disappears as new homes are built on the fields around Barrytown. The space the boys have to play in becomes smaller, and more dangerous, as the novel progresses and Paddy faces more complicated emotional challenges in his life.

Activity 1

1. Look at the quotations below, taken from different points in the novel. Decide what each one tells us about Paddy's growing maturity.

> **Key quotations**
>
> The fire was going well, loads of smoke. I got a stone and threw it at the fire. [...] The coast was clear and he signalled me to come. I charged, crouched down and got to the side of the house. *(page 7)*
>
> Putting two letters in one envelope was stupid. Santy would think it was only one letter and he'd just bring Sinbad's present and not mine. I didn't believe in him anyway. *(page 31)*
>
> Kevin grabbed his arm and twisted it behind his back. [...]
> — He wasn't in the war, said Kevin. — Sure he wasn't?
> — No, said Ian McEvoy. [...]
> — Why did you say he was, then?
> It wasn't fair; he should have let Ian McEvoy go when he'd said No. *(page 196)*
>
> They watched me filling in the day. [...] I wasn't enjoying it. They were all there, and I didn't like them. I was alone. *(page 239)*

2. Keep a list of references to the fields and building sites as you read the novel so that you have an accurate record of the changes. If you keep track of Paddy's games on the same diagram you will be able to compare how Doyle reflects Paddy's growing maturity through his references to the landscape around Barrytown. You might start along these lines:

Fields/Building sites	Games
'We'd go down to the building site [...] There was a new road where there'd been wet cement the last time we were there [...] We went over to where we'd written our names with sticks in the cement, but they'd been smoothed over; they'd gone.' (page 5)	'We lit fires. We were always lighting fires.' (page 4)
	Paddy, Kevin and Liam force lighter fuel into Sinbad's mouth and light it: 'It went like a dragon.' (page 9)
'We escaped, dashed across the remains of the field.' (page 7)	'We spent afternoons burning little piles of cut grass.' (page 9)

Relationships

The theme of relationships is central to the text, with Paddy being part of, or an influence on, a number of them. His parents' marriage, for example, affects the relationship he has with them and the sibling relationship he has with Sinbad, both of which contribute to his home life. His friendships with Kevin and the rest of his gang are also central to Paddy's childhood and the community in which they live: the shrinking nature of their territory mirrors Paddy's increasing isolation, and the boundaries and expectations of adults at school act as a contrast to his family's instability. Throughout all of these environments, power and violence are played out in various types of bullying in which Paddy is sometimes the aggressor and sometimes the victim.

Paddy's parents' marriage is one of the most important relationships in the novel and is written about in detail. Although Paddy is only ten when he narrates the novel, Doyle subtly shows us how the marriage gradually changes through the references that Paddy makes to his parents' behaviour.

Another way that we can see the deterioration of the marriage is through Paddy's references to family routines and, in particular, mealtimes. His parents' arguments are often at mealtimes such as on the picnic, at Sunday breakfast and during the evening meal; on a number of occasions, Paddy hears or sees them arguing when he is on his way to the kitchen for a drink.

This central theme is also explored through Paddy's relationships with his friends and his brother. He recognizes that often his friendships are somewhat **paradoxical** in that they involve both liking and hating people at the same time, which reflects the bewildering nature of growing up.

> **paradox** a contradictory statement

Key quotations

They were our friends because we hated them... *(page 167)*

If you were going to be best friends with anyone – Kevin – you had to hate a lot of other people... *(page 182)*

I went to thump him and before I had a fist made I was crying. [...] I didn't know why I was crying; it shocked me. I let go of his nose. I put my arms around him. *(page 241)*

During the novel we come to see that many of the relationships that people have with one another are not as straightforward as they initially appear:

- Paddy's parents' marriage breaks down.
- Paddy loses Kevin's friendship.

- Sinbad becomes someone to love and protect rather than hate.
- Liam and Aidan's father finds a new partner, Margaret, who moves in with them.
- Mister Hennessey shows Paddy compassion when he falls asleep in class despite usually being a strict disciplinarian.
- Charles Leavy seems to isolate himself on purpose.
- David Geraghty turns out to have a comical and mischievous personality despite being initially disliked and ridiculed by Paddy.

Activity 2

1. Look at the quotations below, taken from different points in the novel. What do they tell us about Paddy's parents' marriage?

> **Key quotations**
>
> **There was a gap and then they burst out laughing, the two of them.** *(page 14)*
>
> **Don't shout at him, Paddy, my ma said to my da, not to us; we weren't supposed to hear it.** *(page 37)*
>
> **My da said nothing. My ma said nothing.** *(page 61)*
>
> **[...] they'd go forward again and it would end for a while. Their fights were like a train that kept getting stuck at the corner tracks and you had to lean over and push it or straighten it.** *(pages 153–154)*
>
> **Then I heard the smack. The talking stopped.** *(page 190)*
>
> **I walked in for a drink of water; I saw her falling back. He looked at me. He unmade his fist. He went red. [...] He looked at her; his hands moved. I thought he was going to put her back to where she'd been before he hit her.** *(page 280)*

There are two comments, in particular, that you could make about the presentation of Paddy's parents' marriage from the above quotations. One is the fact that the arguing develops into physical aggression. The other one is more subtle and reflects Doyle's skill as a storyteller – the apparently unconnected comments Paddy makes about the laughter changing to talking, which changes to silence and then to violence.

Look for other quotations about the marriage and see if they fit into the same pattern.

2. Why do you think Doyle sets so many of Paddy's parents' arguments around mealtimes?

Violence

The paradox of love/hate is often conveyed through violence, another strong thematic thread in the novel. Many of the characters are either an aggressor (such as Paddy's father) or a victim of violence (for example, his mother), or even (like Paddy) one or the other at differing points in the novel.

Key quotations

I'll crucify you.

James O'Keefe's ma always said that to James O'Keefe and his brothers and sister. All she meant was Do what you're told. I'll leather you. I'll skin you alive. I'll break every bone in your body. I'll tear you limb from limb. I'll maim you. [...] I'll swing for you. [...]

My ma explained.

— It means that she'll murder him and then she'll be condemned to hang for it but she doesn't really mean it.

— Why doesn't she say what she does mean?

— It's just the way people talk. *(pages 206–207)*

Violence is used as a form of punishment by teachers in the novel

Activity 3

Violence is perpetrated in all sorts of environments in the novel and in some cases, such as school, is actually an acceptable form of punishment (known as corporal punishment). Copy and complete the spider diagram below to show the various types of violence and who experiences it.

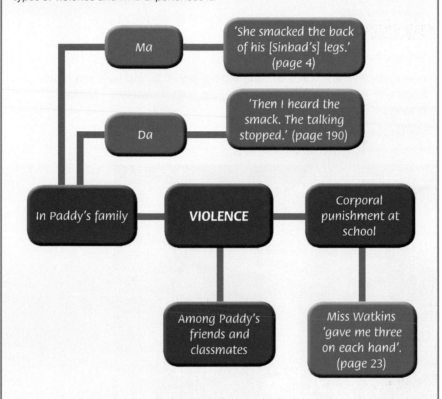

School and learning

The routines and discipline of school can be seen as a contrast to the increasing disorder of Paddy's home life: eccer (homework) has to be completed; there are set lessons and breaks; and even Mister Hennessey's comments have a predictability to them.

Key quotations

— Twenty-nine past ten, Sir.

— What day is it, Mister O'Connell?

— Thursday, Sir.

— Are you sure?

— Yes, Sir.

We laughed.

— It is Wednesday, I'm told, said Henno. And it is half past ten. What book will we now take out of our *málas*, Mister – Mister – Mister O'Keefe?

We laughed. We had to. *(page 265)*

The predictability and routine of the classroom gives order to Paddy's life

Although Paddy does not appear to have a positive or negative view of school, he is interested in the world around him. He questions his father about the newspaper headline 'World War Three Looms Near', visits the library regularly, asks his mother questions such as why a 'drawing room' isn't for drawing in and, when watching the news, asks his father, **'Why are the yankees fighting the gorillas?'** *(page 227)*. However, this inquisitiveness also heightens Paddy's isolation as it makes him aware of Kevin's shortcomings as a friend and that there is something gravely wrong with his parents' relationship.

Writing about themes

Upgrade

- Remember that themes run like threads through a novel, although they may get stronger or weaker as the narrative progresses. You should be able to track the development of a theme, rather than just writing about blocks of unconnected events.
- Don't shy away from commenting on a theme's increasing or decreasing significance. It shows you have knowledge of the whole book if you are able to write about a difference between the beginning and the end.
- Don't be put off if the exam question asks you about the theme of 'growing up' rather than 'childhood', for example. Make sure you know all the terms that are relevant to the themes in the novel and be aware of subtle differences. Don't try to make what you know well fit into a different question.
- Make links between themes to show that you understand that they are connected.

Exam skills

Unpicking the question

Although you cannot know what is going to appear on your exam paper, particular words and phrases are frequently used in exam questions. Look at the sample questions below.

> **Comment on / Discuss / Explain** the importance of relationships in the novel.

When answering this type of question, you need to write about the topic in detail, focusing on its role in the novel rather than giving a commentary on where it appears and which characters are involved. In relation to *Paddy Clarke Ha Ha Ha*, you might write about how Paddy's friendship with Kevin is central to the narrative structure of the novel and also how it acts as a **metaphor** for Paddy's journey towards adulthood. A thorough answer will contain a discussion about a variety of relationships.

> **metaphor** a comparison of one thing with another to make a description more vivid; a metaphor states that one thing *is* the other

> **Explore / Examine** Doyle's presentation of friendship in the novel.

This asks you to look very carefully at a particular topic, considering a variety of viewpoints. You need to be extremely familiar with the text to pick out relevant examples and discuss them in detail rather than making vague references to several episodes. Again, avoid giving a narrative account of events; instead consider contrasts and comparisons.

> **How** does Doyle show both humour and sadness in this extract? / **Show how** Doyle creates both humour and sadness in this extract.

'How' questions are asking you to comment on the author's technique, or craft. You need to consider the effectiveness of Doyle's writing and analyse what he does with the text. You must be alert to the effects of Doyle's language and the way he makes his characters behave in the extract. You must also be able to illustrate his techniques by giving relevant quotations or examples.

> How is Paddy's father **portrayed / presented** in the novel?

This question is really asking, 'How is this shown to us?' or 'What has the author done that makes us feel a certain way about this character or event?' Strong answers, in this example, will look at the way in which Doyle has Paddy tell us about some of the enjoyable times he has spent with his father and the fact that he is confused as to why his parents are arguing. There are hints right from the start of the novel that his father is easily angered, but Doyle shows us that he is more than a one-dimensional bully.

> What **role** does Charles Leavy play in the novel?

This is not an opportunity to tell the examiner what the character does in the novel but to consider why Doyle has written him into the text in a particular way. For example, why does Charles Leavy appear two-thirds of the way through the novel? What is his purpose? What does he represent?

> **What makes** this extract such a tense moment in the novel?

This is asking you to examine the writer's craft. It requires careful study of the text and you need to pick out and analyse a variety of the techniques the author has used to create the effect.

> **Write about** the relationship between Paddy and his group of friends.

You need to comment on, or examine, the topic in the question. Look beyond the narrative at how the topic is presented, how it changes (if at all) and its significance through the novel.

Look at the question below. The key words and phrases have been highlighted and explained.

Give my opinion and also consider how other readers might view the character.

How Doyle makes us have these opinions; what he does in his writing to make us think as we do.

> What do you think of Kevin and the way he is presented?

Kevin: as a friend to Paddy and the gang; as a child; his role in the novel.

Activity 1

Look at the exam questions below. With a partner, decide what the key words are in each question. Then write a list of things you need to do to answer each question.

> What do you think of Charles Leavy and his presentation in the novel?

> How do you think Paddy changes towards the end of the novel?

> Explore Paddy and Sinbad's changing relationship.

> How does Doyle's writing make the picnic scene a powerful moment?

Planning your answer

In the exam, it is important to give yourself a moment to think about your answer before you start writing it. Spend five minutes planning your answer so that your ideas are organized into a well-developed, structured response.

Below are several ways that you can write a plan. Experiment with different methods and decide which works best for you.

Lists

You can list points that you want to include, perhaps with a brief note of the evidence you will use. This is what the list for the following question might look like:

> **Explore the presentation of community in *Paddy Clarke Ha Ha Ha*.**

- ✔ Introduction: Barrytown community: Paddy's family, friends, neighbours, school, Corporation homes, church.
- ✔ Paddy knows lots of neighbours, as he misbehaves in their gardens, and lots of people interact with him and his friends outside the home.
- ✔ Doyle never refers to other children or adults being in the house. There are lots of references to slamming doors when his parents argue and when his father leaves: possibly a metaphor for the saying, 'behind closed doors'.
- ✔ As the new Corporation houses are built Doyle refers to the fields 'disappearing' and Paddy and his friends are unwelcoming to the new children.
- ✔ In many ways they are unhappy in their community: Ma doesn't like Kevin's mother or the language Paddy picks up (e.g. 'Slum scum').
- ✔ Conclusion: although initially Doyle suggested that this is an established and happy community, by the end we realize it is disappearing along with Paddy's childhood.

Spider diagrams

You could also put your points into a spider diagram like this, adding more ideas if you wish.

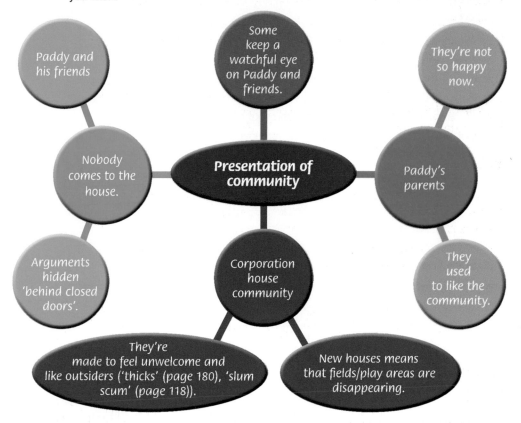

Writing your answer

A good plan will help you to organize your ideas in a logical structure in your essay. Your answer should show your knowledge and understanding of:

- what the writer is saying
- how the writer is saying it
- how the setting and context influence the writer and reader (where relevant).

Quotations and PEE (Point, Evidence, Explanation)

Examiners want to see you use quotations as evidence of your understanding, but you need to ensure they are relevant to what you are writing. Using PEE will help you to make precise and relevant points, use appropriate evidence and analyse and explain the effect it has. For example:

Point: Paddy is bewildered by his parents' rows and what causes them.

Evidence: 'I didn't understand. She was lovely. He was nice. They had four children.'

Explanation: Paddy's simple assertions and short sentences show that he is confused and unable to connect their current actions with his perception of them and their role as parents. This might make the reader sad for Paddy because we can see that as a child he does not understand the complexities of his parents' relationship. It might also make us feel angry because he seemed so carefree at the beginning of the novel, as shown through humorous anecdotes, whereas now he is constantly anxious about his parents and family.

If you can embed your quotations, you will provide a more fluent answer. For example, look at this exam question:

Explore how Doyle presents education and learning in the novel.

In answering this question, you might want to include the first time that Mister Hennessey is mentioned to show that school seems an unfair place because the teacher clearly does not like some of the children. For example, you could write:

We know that Mister Hennessey does not like James O'Keefe because Paddy tells us:

'The master, Mister Hennessey, hated James O'Keefe. [...] he'd say, — O'Keefe, I know you're up to something down there. [...] He said it one morning and James O'Keefe wasn't even in.'

This shows that the boys are subjected to unfair treatment and, although the reader might find it funny, it hints at a bullying atmosphere in school.

Although this is fine, as it adequately fulfils PEE, a more fluent answer would use an embedded quotation like this:

We know that Mister Hennessey does not like James O'Keefe because Paddy tells us that the teacher assumed it was O'Keefe misbehaving at the back of the class even when he was 'at home with the mumps' which, although a humorous anecdote for the reader, hints at a bullying atmosphere at school.

Activity 2

With a partner, choose one of the sample questions on page 66.

a) Together, write a plan to answer the question.

b) Decide, between you, on some relevant quotations to help you answer the question.

c) Individually, write a PEE paragraph using a relevant quotation.

d) Share your paragraphs to consider what you have both done well and what could be improved.

e) Repeat the activity with another sample question.

What to do in an exam answer

✔ Make sure you are prepared: know what the time limits are and understand the type of question you will be asked.

✔ Read the questions carefully, highlighting or underlining important words or phrases.

✔ Take a few minutes to write a plan to help you organize your thoughts. If necessary, rearrange points before committing them to your final answer.

✔ Write a brief introduction of only one or two sentences to give an overview of your answer and lead fluently to your first point.

✔ Write about your strongest point in the first paragraph and try to link each subsequent paragraph with words and phrases such as 'However', 'Later in the novel', 'This is further suggested by', 'Despite this we see', and 'This contradicts'.

✔ Include a conclusion that summarizes the points you've made. It only needs to be a couple of sentences but it is a sign of a developed and rounded response.

What not to do in an exam answer

✘ Do not answer questions on the wrong text.

✘ Do not answer all questions if you are supposed to make a choice.

✘ Do not write an introduction that begins 'In this essay I will show you…' and merely repeats the question.

✘ Do not refer to the author as Roddy or Mr Doyle.

✘ When answering an extract question, do not concentrate on one section of the extract and ignore the rest of it.

✘ Do not overrun on time limits; move on once the time for that particular question is up.

✘ Do not write down everything you know about the novel or everything you know about Roddy Doyle. Your points should be relevant to the question asked.

Sample questions

1

Foundation Tier

Paddy Clarke Ha Ha Ha

Either a)

Look at the extract on page 190 from 'The first time I heard it...' to 'Across the face.'

What do you think makes this such a powerful moment in the novel?

You should consider:

- what Paddy hears
- how his parents react
- the words and phrases Doyle uses.

Or b)

What impression do you get of the way Paddy's parents' marriage changes during the novel?

Remember to support your ideas with details from the novel.

2

Higher Tier

Paddy Clarke Ha Ha Ha

Either a)

Look at the extract on page 190 from 'The first time I heard it...' to 'Across the face.'

How does Doyle's writing make this a powerful and significant moment in the novel?

Or b)

How does Doyle vividly convey the change in Paddy's parents' relationship in the course of the novel?

Remember to support your ideas with details from the novel.

3

Foundation Tier

Paddy Clarke Ha Ha Ha

Answer part (a) and **either** part (b) **or** part (c).

(a) *Look at the extract on pages 281–282 from 'Paddy Clarke –' to 'Very well, thank you.'*

What are your thoughts and feelings as you read this extract? Give reasons for what you say and remember to support your answer with words and phrases from the extract.

Either

(b) What do you think about Charles Leavy?
Think about:
- his relationships with other characters
- how others, including Paddy, view him
- the way he speaks and behaves at different times in the novel.

Or

(c) What is your impression of Barrytown?
Think about:
- the people who live there
- some of the events that Roddy Doyle writes about
- the way Paddy describes the town
- anything else you think is important.

4

Higher Tier

Paddy Clarke Ha Ha Ha

Answer part (a) and **either** part (b) **or** part (c).

(a) *Look at the extract on pages 281–282 from 'Paddy Clarke –' to 'Very well, thank you.'*

With close reference to the extract, show how Roddy Doyle creates a powerful ending here.

Either

(b) What do you think of Charles Leavy and the way he is presented in the novel?

Or

(c) How does Roddy Doyle present the town of Barrytown in *Paddy Clarke Ha Ha Ha*?

Achieving the best marks

Upgrade

To get good marks, you will need to do the following:

- Explore the text perceptively and thoughtfully.
- Write with insight about links between the text and its context, and the importance of the text to readers in different times and places.
- Show sensitive understanding of the significance and effects of Doyle's choices of language, structure and form.
- Give a pertinent and fluent response to the question.
- Select relevant evidence that is securely embedded in your response.

In order to do all this, you need to do more than read the set text. Try to read some of Doyle's other novels to give you more of an idea of his usual writing style, the settings for his books and how he presents characters. Read critical guides too, if you can, and think about others' opinions of Doyle's writing. Although you will not need (or have time) to include these in your exam answers, it will give you a much better overview of the type of writer that Doyle is, how other people respond to his writing, and the reasons for their opinions.

You need to show that you have understood the novel on more than the level of a poignant, and yet humorous, tale of a boy growing up with parents in a failing marriage. It's also the story of lost innocence, a changing community, the bewildering nature of growing up and the horror and shame of domestic violence behind closed doors.

You will need to show your understanding of why Doyle chose Paddy as his narrator, what the effect is of having the child's viewpoint and how the structure of the narrative is effective. Consider, as well, why Doyle writes about Irish settings that are familiar to him and what you think his opinion might be about the changing landscape of suburban communities such as the fictional Barrytown.

In addition, you need to write fluently, clearly and convincingly, and with relevant literary terminology that reflects a sophisticated understanding of the novel and the author's craft.

Sample answers

Sample answer 1

Below you will find a sample response from a **Foundation Tier** student, together with examiner comments, to the following question:

> Why is Kevin such an important character in the story?
> You should consider:
>
> - his role in Paddy's friendship group
> - his influence on Paddy
> - his behaviour at the end of the novel.

A strong assertion, but a lot of Paddy's anxieties are to do with wanting to be Kevin's best friend.

Excellent point about Kevin's role in the novel.

Kevin is the leader of the gang and Paddy's best friend. He is in charge of his friends and makes them do what he says. Throughout the book Kevin stays the same whereas Paddy changes, so Kevin represents childhood in comparison to Paddy's increasing maturity. At the end of the book he is no longer Paddy's friend, is unkind to him and turns everyone else against him.

Repetition.

Kevin is the leader of the boys' gang and Paddy's best friend. This can be seen at the opening of the novel when Paddy says, 'We were coming down our road. Kevin stopped at a gate and bashed it with his stick.' The use of 'we' without introduction shows that the boys are good friends.

Use of the word 'wants' highlights the imbalance in the friendship.

This point needs developing much more: there is a lot that can be said about Kevin's power over Paddy.

Paddy is impressed by Kevin through most of the novel and wants to be his best friend. Even when Paddy knows an answer to a question, if Kevin is there, 'I never rushed with an answer, in school or anywhere; I always gave him a chance to answer first.' This is because he admires Kevin so much that he does not want to seem cleverer than him even though, as readers, we realize he probably is.

Good: shows recognition that there is a change in the relationship.

Towards the end of the book, however, Paddy realizes that Kevin is not such a good friend. He tells us, after lying to Kevin about his parents' rows, 'I'd escaped' because Paddy suddenly recognizes that Kevin would gossip.

Makes a pertinent point about Kevin's role in the novel's structure, but needs much more development.

In a way, Kevin represents childhood in the novel: both at the beginning and at the end he is seen doing very childish activities. At the beginning he is banging Missis Quigley's gate and at the end he sends David Geraghty to hit Paddy with one of his crutches.

Good attempt to summarize the points made.

Makes a new point (sweeping generalization) that should not be in the conclusion.

Kevin is an important character throughout the novel because he is Paddy's best friend, he illustrates how much Paddy changes in contrast to himself who does not change at all and he can be seen as a typical Irish child of the 1960s.

Sample answer 2

The sample answer below is from a **Higher Tier** student to the following question:

> Why is Kevin such an important character in the story?

Kevin's importance stems from his position as undisputed leader of Paddy's friendship group, Paddy's constant longing to be his best friend through most of the novel, his childishness which acts as a contrast to Paddy's growing maturity, and his involvement in all of the games that he, Paddy and the others play which might be seen as a representation of an Irish childhood in the late 1960s.

Strong introduction clearly summarizes Kevin's importance.

Excellent vocabulary concisely identifies Kevin's role.

Recognizes that the friendship is not equal.

Addresses context well.

Kevin is clearly important to Paddy and we see his influence over him on a number of occasions: when Paddy confides to us that he always gives Kevin a chance to answer questions first even if he knows the answer; that he is 'delighted' when Seán Whelan is sat next to Liam as he thinks he and Kevin will not speak to Liam again, 'There was just me and Kevin now, no one else'; and he even pretends that he supported Kevin over the chanting game when the others will not play again unless Kevin takes his turn. All these examples display Kevin's power over Paddy through most of the novel and even reveal Paddy's fear of losing Kevin's friendship. Doyle lets us in on Paddy's naive awe of Kevin and lets us, as readers, see the reality by using phrases such as, 'I never rushed with an answer, in school or anywhere; I always gave him a chance to answer first' so that we can see that Paddy is, in all likelihood, cleverer than Kevin.

Use of an embedded quotation gives fluency to the response.

Shows understanding of Doyle as the writer and how he presents ideas.

This analysis of the quotation could be clearer and needs developing.

This idolization of Kevin through most of the book is in stark contrast to Paddy's changed feelings near the end when he has been boycotted by the gang and tells us that Kevin, 'wasn't my friend any more. He was a sap, a spoofer and a liar. He hadn't a clue.' Paddy's list of harsh insults here reflects the change that he has undergone; he has matured, has become cynical about Kevin's position and recognizes that Kevin does not understand life beyond his own childhood. Throughout the novel Kevin has been an illustration of a childhood untouched by adult anxieties. He shows the reader what Paddy might have been like if he had not been so sensitive to his parents' unhappiness.

Strong exploration of the point just made above, it develops the idea and reflects the candidate's ability to consider possibilities about the text.

Addresses context but is a generalization; it needs modification such as, 'It could/might be an illustration...' or 'It is possibly Doyle's recollection of...'

In danger of drifting away from focus but avoids this by only commenting on Kevin's background.

Not addressed in the main part of the essay.

Summarizes Kevin's importance in the structure of the novel as well as the story.

The games that we see Paddy and all his friends involved in, on the shrinking playground of fields, are an illustration to us of a childhood in the Republic of Ireland in the late 1960s. Kevin and the rest of the friends might be seen as representations of different aspects of society; each has a small back story that we glimpse as readers. Kevin's parents own their own home; have an older son who is often in trouble and apparently intends to join the FCA (the voluntary part-time Army Reserve); and they refer to other people with insults such as 'Slum scum'. Kevin tells Paddy quite openly that they have arguments, 'They have them all the time' and it can be assumed from his manner and tone that he sees this as quite a normal activity for parents.

Doyle portrays Kevin as a young boy with bullying tendencies, who is insensitive to the troubles of others. His rather cruel behaviour is a contrast to Paddy's increasingly mature outlook and understanding. Kevin and his family are also important to the narrative structure: being both a part of the many anecdotes Paddy tells and giving us a glimpse into another 1960s' Irish childhood in the same increasingly suburban environment.

Sample answer 3

Read the extract below taken from a student response, together with examiner comments, to the following sample **Foundation Tier** question:

> Read the extract from pages 142–143 from 'My da wouldn't let us have a dog…' to 'But he stayed on his legs and straightened and ran to the side of the house, to the front.'
>
> What impressions of Paddy do you have when you read this extract?

At this point in the story, and from this episode, Paddy seems to be a fairly typical ten-year-old boy.

Does not introduce the essay's points and would make a better opening if the second paragraph was joined here.

He wants to have a dog of his own, and relays his disappointment that his Dad will not let him have one, but then describes in detail his and Kevin's cruelty to Benson. Through this Doyle illustrates that Paddy is still immature as he does not make the connection between his own meanness and not being allowed a dog of his own.

Recognizes Doyle crafting the episode.

Although Paddy and Kevin are equally unkind to Benson (and Ian McEvoy), we get a sense of Paddy's underlying fears when he confesses to us his worries that Benson will die: 'a terror screamed through me, up through me'. Although he does not say any of this out loud, Doyle's use of 'screamed through me' tells us that Paddy has a rising and uncontrollable fear that is only stopped when Benson runs off.

Makes a good attempt to analyse Doyle's use of language but the understanding is implicit and the vocabulary choices need to be explored in more detail.

Paddy's anxieties about imagining a terrible future are also shown when he thinks that, 'Blood would come out of his mouth'; this is like his fears about his parents' marriage in that the anxieties about what might happen keep him awake at night.

Makes a good attempt to link Paddy's behaviour to other parts of the novel but the connection is not particularly well made.

Paddy's childish ways are clearly seen in this extract with his almost forensic interest in Benson's tail: 'the tail was a bone, a hairy bone', his worry of making sure his 'free fingers didn't touch his bum' and the casual remark to us that sometimes he only pretends to wash his hands before dinner.

Excellent use of vocabulary clearly shows Paddy's behaviour.

Point needs development. Why does Paddy say this? How does it affect our impression of him?

Overall, in this extract, we get the impression of Paddy as a typical young boy, but we also see hints of his anxieties about the future.

Makes a good attempt at a conclusion but is slightly repetitious.

Sample answer 4

Read the extract below taken from a student response, together with examiner comments, to the following sample **Higher Tier** question:

> How does Doyle present childhood in the novel?

Strong introduction clearly summarizes the ways in which Doyle presents childhood.

Through the voice of Paddy as ten-year-old narrator, and all that he experiences, Doyle makes childhood key to the novel. Doyle presents childhood in the following, often contrasting, ways: Paddy with his friends; the constraints of school; the loss of innocence that Paddy experiences as he realizes his parents' marriage is failing; the different backgrounds of the children; Paddy himself changing, maturing and then looking back on friendships he no longer covets.

This is repetition and unnecessary.

Childhood, and Paddy's experiences of it, is central to the novel. The opening scene is Paddy and Kevin, both ten, 'coming down our road' bashing Missis Quigley's gate with a stick. The sense of ownership of the environment is key to Doyle's portrayal. The fields and building sites around Paddy's home are described as Paddy and his friends' 'territory'. Throughout the novel and through all the escapades of racing through neighbours' gardens, running through the new drainage system, hiding in the barn, tramping down nettles and building dens, the reader gets the sense of the children as the centre of the community and all adults, and outsiders, as being unimportant and on the periphery of their world.

Very good, close analysis of Doyle's language.

Gives a comprehensive list of examples as evidence.

Phrase shows strong development.

School, in contrast to these freedoms, shows a different aspect of childhood. In Doyle's novel, school is a place of rigidity and conformity where the boys march, chant and learn facts by rote. Paddy's teacher, Mister Hennessey, is very strict. At the beginning Paddy tells us that Mister Hennessey does not like James O'Keefe, telling him off even when he's absent with mumps. By the end of the novel, though, Paddy has realized that Mister Hennessey is often unfair: when he picks on his brother Sinbad just for crying and in the last scene in which we see Mister Hennessey, Paddy tells us that when the teacher is picking on someone publically, 'We laughed. We had to' as if Paddy has recognized how the child/teacher relationship works.

This could be an interesting point about adults behaving in a childish way but it remains an inference here.

A very pertinent quotation but the explanation of it needs development as the final sentence is too vague.

This growing awareness of how relationships work is also central to Paddy's growing maturity and his journey away from childhood.

His relationship with Kevin is key in that at the beginning, and through most of the novel, he is most keen to be Kevin's best friend and is even 'delighted' when Seán Whelan is sat next to Liam as he feels this cements his own friendship with Kevin. However, he becomes increasingly aware of Kevin's often cruel and apparently arbitrary way of choosing his friends. At the beginning of the novel, Doyle lets the reader deduce this from such remarks as Paddy commenting that he does not answer a question if Kevin is there and also that Kevin gives Sinbad a Chinese burn and taunts him when he is stuck in a hedge. However, later on, Paddy himself tells us that Kevin behaves unfairly when he continues to keep Ian McEvoy in an arm lock despite his capitulation over a lie. At the close of the novel, Paddy is unbothered by the loss of Kevin's friendship and the cruel chants from his childhood friends, telling us, 'I didn't listen to them. They were only kids.' We can see he has distanced himself from them and no longer sees himself as part of their gang. Paddy is now quite isolated and alone as he moves into adulthood, particularly as his father has left home and Paddy views himself as 'the man of the house'.

Paddy's change has come quite subtly and it is only when we look back through the novel that we see that Doyle first presents us with a group of boys who all seem fairly similar: running rather wild, misbehaving, playing football and building dens, but then they all become much more individual, each having their own personality and back story. Kevin, for example, has an older brother who is often in trouble; Liam and Aidan's mother is dead, and Paddy describes their home life in some detail, feeling rather uncomfortable that their father has to do all the cooking and cleaning as well as working. Charles Leavy, who Paddy comes to idolize for his isolation, is presented as impoverished and uncared for; Edward Swanwick appears to come from a more middle-class home and is sent to a different school (possibly independent), where they wear blazers and play rugby.

Doyle presents childhood as it is: many different experiences to different people. He shows us the freedoms of late 1960s' Ireland in the fields but also the contrasts of 1960s' education in which learning was by rote and often dull and uninspiring. Paddy's own childhood is portrayed as a journey which we witness: from the innocent, unquestioning arrogance of seeing himself as the centre of his environment to the recognition that life, and those in it, are often cruel and behave badly, and his own increasing bewilderment and then isolation as he deals with these situations.

Excellent point shows clear understanding of how Doyle uses Paddy's narrative voice to give the reader a particular perspective on a scene.

Makes a strong point but only implies how we can see that Paddy has distanced himself.

Quotation really needs explanation rather than being left at the end of the paragraph.

Good point recognizes different and changing interpretations of the novel.

List of different characters needs more development to show how and why Doyle might have included all these children.

Highlights the context of the novel.

Strong closing sentence summarizes how Doyle presents childhood.

Glossary

analogy a comparison which highlights similarities

anecdote a short story about an incident or person, which is particularly interesting or amusing

aside a speech in a play given by an actor directly to the audience, unheard by the other characters

autobiographical writing the story of a person's life written by themselves

chronological narrative the presentation of events in a story in the order in which they actually occurred

colloquialism a word or phrase that is informal or non-standard and often characteristic of a particular region or country

colloquial language informal, everyday speech

coming-of-age novel a literary genre focused on the main character's psychological and moral growth

eponymous the person after whom something is named

first-person narrative a story told from the narrator's point of view, using the pronoun 'I' or 'me'

hierarchy a system that ranks people or groups according to status

infer to guess something based on evidence

irony the discrepancy between what a character could be expected to do and what they actually do, often for comic effect

juxtaposition various things or ideas placed side by side to highlight the differences between them

linear narrative the presentation of events in a story in the order in which they actually occurred

metaphor a comparison of one thing with another to make a description more vivid; a metaphor states that one thing *is* the other

narrator the person who tells a story (Paddy is the narrator in *Paddy Clarke Ha Ha Ha*)

paradox a contradictory statement

protagonist the central character in a novel

register a variety of language used in a particular setting; the degree of language formality

retrospective narrative a narrative relating events that happened in the narrator's past

stereotype a common but overly simplified view of a particular type of person

symbolism using something to represent a concept, idea or theme in a novel

verbatim reported word for word

vignette a short, descriptive sketch that creates an impression of a character, setting or concept

OXFORD
UNIVERSITY PRESS

Great Clarendon Street, Oxford OX2 6DP

Oxford University Press is a department of the University of Oxford.
It furthers the University's objective of excellence in research,
scholarship, and education by publishing worldwide in

Oxford   New York

Auckland   Cape Town   Dar es Salaam   Hong Kong   Karachi
Kuala Lumpur   Madrid   Melbourne   Mexico City   Nairobi
New Delhi   Shanghai   Taipei   Toronto

With offices in

Argentina   Austria   Brazil   Chile   Czech Republic   France   Greece
Guatemala   Hungary   Italy   Japan   Poland   Portugal   Singapore
South Korea   Switzerland   Thailand   Turkey   Ukraine   Vietnam

Oxford is a registered trade mark of Oxford University Press
in the UK and in certain other countries

© Mary Williamson 2012

The moral rights of the author have been asserted

Database right Oxford University Press (maker)

First published 2012

All rights reserved. No part of this publication may be reproduced,
stored in a retrieval system, or transmitted, in any form or by any means,
without the prior permission in writing of Oxford University Press, or as
expressly permitted by law, or under terms agreed with the appropriate
reprographics rights organization. Enquiries concerning reproduction
outside the scope of the above should be sent to the Rights Department,
Oxford University Press, at the address above

You must not circulate this book in any other binding or cover
and you must impose this same condition on any acquirer

British Library Cataloguing in Publication Data

Data available

ISBN 978-0-19-912876-1

10 9 8 7 6 5 4 3 2 1

Printed in Great Britain by Bell and Bain Ltd., Glasgow

Acknowledgements
The publisher and author are grateful for permission to reprint the
following copyright material:

Extracts from Roddy Doyle: *Paddy Clarke Ha Ha Ha* (Secker & Warburg,
1993), copyright © Roddy Doyle 1993, reprinted by permission of The
Random House Group Ltd.

Cover: Nick Yapp/Getty Images

p6: Harald Theissen/Alamy; **p14:** Ruggiero.S/Shutterstock; **p16:** Pegaz/Alamy; **p19:** INTERFOTO/
Alamy; **p24:** jeremy sutton-hibbert/Alamy; **p26:** Bettmann/Corbis; **p28t:** A. F. Archive/Alamy;
p28b: Associated Sports Photography/Shutterstock; **p30:** David Bromley/Shutterstock; **p33:** Tengku
Mohd Yusof bin Tg. Su/Shutterstock; **p35:** Sarah Cates/Shutterstock; **p41:** Farrell Grehan/Corbis;
p51: ClassicStock/Corbis; **p55:** The Art Archive/Alamy; **p56:** Christine Spengler/Corbis; **p60:** Kunz
Wolfgang/Alamy; **p62:** Mirrorpix/Alamy.

Illustrations by Barking Dog

BARTON PEVERIL
COLLEGE LIBRARY
EASTLEIGH SO50 5ZA